THE BEATLES

Enzo Gentile
Fabio Schiavo

in Comic Strips

SKIRA

Cover
Rock Legends: The Beatles, Pop
Comics, Whitney Publishing Company,
USA, 1995

Back Cover
Lupo Alberto. Almanacco del Rock,
Macchia Nera S.R.L., Italy, 1993
Detail of back cover

Design
Marcello Francone

Editorial Coordination
Vincenza Russo

Editing
Doriana Comerlati

Layout
Anna Cattaneo
Giulia Ferrazzi

Translations
Christopher Evans for Language
Consulting Congressi, Milan

Iconographical Research
Alessandra Mion

First published in Italy in 2012 by
Skira Editore S.p.A.
Palazzo Casati Stampa
via Torino 61
20123 Milano
Italy
www.skira.net

© 2012 Skira editore

Printed and bound in Italy. First edition

ISBN: 978-88-572-0811-4

Distributed in USA, Canada, Central
& South America by Rizzoli
International Publications, Inc.,
300 Park Avenue South, New York,
NY 10010, USA.
Distributed elsewhere in the world
by Thames and Hudson Ltd., 181A
High Holborn, London WC1V 7QX,
United Kingdom.

I would like to thank the god of music,
who has given me insatiable antennae,
taste buds and sonic desire; men and
women of goodwill, my family, friends,
teachers and loves; the passion and
emotion of those who have stood behind
me. And will continue to do so to the end.
e.

Lucia, my wife, for the patience she has
shown in putting up with a house invaded
by mountains of paper, my son Roberto for
reading the comic strips without destroying
them, Maffialife for the website, Riccardo
Mazzoni, Luigi and Melina, Rick Bradford,
Jaudidudi, Alejandro Leoncio! and all those
who have helped me to find comics
I would otherwise never have heard of.
To many others I cock a heartfelt snook.
f.

www.thebeatlescomics.com

THE BEATLES

di
Raffaele Ciccaleni

LATO SIDE EDITORI

Contents

Is It Tomorrow or Just the End of Time?

Enzo Gentile

Heroes, the real ones, don't grow old, they're never tired—indeed, to quote the words of a song, "heroes are forever young and handsome." And so what could be better than a life in comic strips to immortalize a myth, to make it even clearer that The Beatles have been every bit an otherworldly creature *as well*, suspended, after the awesome planetwide success of the sixties, in a sort of bubble outside time? Turning them into cartoons, ageless figures and symbols, without wrinkles or stretch marks, and even phenomena impossible to tarnish through their own art—a theoretically foolhardy venture, as it was undertaken when the foursome were already at the height of their career. We are now more aware of this than ever, as their story has been marked by a series of anniversaries, and The Beatles are (still) an extraordinary totem: a full fifty years after they took their first steps, forty since the game came to an end, thirty since the tragic murder of John Lennon, who would have celebrated his seventieth birthday in October 2010. A hypothetical boomerang, to be projected into a comic strip when they had already stopped writing songs and as solo artists had come up with some not very successful pieces? Not a bit of it! Inadmissible fantasies: paper leaves no room for problems like these. The Beatles *über alles*, outside the rules, always and forever!

Thinking about it, the comic strip is the best formula for The Beatles, the ideal place for them to play a leading role, without too many complications, in the rooms of our daily lives. Comic books at the most may get a little crumpled, but who is going to look at the date of their publication, something that is instead necessary and obligatory for any other journal or magazine? A strip cannot become outdated, unlike a piece of news, a comment, a photograph of this or that starlet. Being made into a comic strip has been and remains a sort of life insurance, a one-way trip to glory, independent of the calendar.

Of course, to become part of that universe, to arrive in it, to be immortalized in a strip, is not something that you can aim for or desire. Those fortunate few to which it has happened—and among their contemporaries in flesh and blood The Beatles soundly trounce the competition in this field too, being documented in the market of the cartoon, uninterruptedly, from their advent to our own day— are grateful for the circumstances and the conditions that have made it possible. And from those pages continue to smile and sing in silence, as spotless as the finest of memories.

It is their story, and history, their beauty, and there's nothing we can do about it: except perhaps look at it, given that the selection of strips reproduced here testifies to a truly extraordinary breadth of imagination (in quantity and quality), that would never have been suspected by the legions of Beatles fans who grew up to the soundtrack that emerged first from Liverpool and then from Abbey Road.

Being turned into a symbol, a character, a point of reference in the world of comics counts only if you haven't sought it and haven't chosen it. The little big heroes that all of us have—Mickey Mouse, Goofy, Batman, Buck Rogers, the Phantom or Spider-Man...—were born out of the ingenuity, the inventiveness of their "pencil-wielding parents," while The Beatles have been modified in parallel to a legendary career that the comic strip has helped to underline and to colour. With each author and cartoonist adding a touch of his own, a dash to the physiognomy of the characters, broadening the spectrum of affection, liking and gratitude towards our idols.

From a phenomenon of the record industry and show business, The Beatles have been able to go a step further, toward global entertainment, thanks both to their music and to their faces, attitudes, clothes and dialogue (as seen in/taken from the films of Richard Lester). And so their appearance in the pages of cartoonists was a logical consequence of a universal popularity, without bounds or reservations. Even before entering Madame Tussauds wax museum or arriving on the big screen (the Fab Four in cinemascope!), The Beatles had begun to travel, who knows how unconsciously, as a natural comic strip. On the one hand the singles and LPs, making up a soundtrack resistant to every shift in fashion, on the other their adventures in comics all over the world, presenting an illuminating vision impervious to events—malleable, to be handled without crumpling, a psychedelic and ever-changing metamorphosis, leading to the final destination of absolute icon, able to withstand any quirks of the weather.

Product and cause of a fame without equals in the history of the society of the spectacle, The Beatles were at once to be centrifuged in the blender of modern pop culture, reverberating and swirling in the funnel of history and coming back into circulation in newspaper reports and many other formats under everyone's eyes, at the centre of a frenzy of media merchandising that can be summed up in a single word, one of boundless power, Beatlemania, at once centre of gravity and sublime cosmic projection.

In any case the exploits of John, Paul, George and Ringo were semantically already clear, running parallel to the popularity achieved through records and songs engraved like a tattoo on our memory. When they received honours from the queen or went to India, when they crossed swords on the set of the films *Help!* and *A Hard Day's Night* or sang "I Am the Walrus" (1967), it was evident that they belonged to another segment of the world of communication, ready to make the leap into another solar system. A mass-media miracle, typical of The Beatles...

And even developments touched by the shadow of death—bizarre rumour when the news spread that Paul had been killed in a road accident and replaced by a double, or terrible reality when John would be mowed down by four bullets outside his house—brought The Beatles back into that territory between fiction and dream where the comic strip can serve as a supplement, as a seasoning of spice, in support of an uncontested phenomenology, even more spectacular and astounding, in Technicolor. Champions of a horizontal language, inscribed by rights in the open field of fantasy and the most unbridled imagination precisely thanks to this virtuoso capacity of distributing themselves all over the place in the world of media production, The Beatles already represented in the golden years—those unique, sensational sixties—a magnificent, fluorescent tapestry beyond space and the calendar. They expressed themselves, standing out from the everyday, with the faces, the grimaces, the declarations, the classical hyperbole of comic-strip heroes: a different dimension, cutting across and foreign to that of all their colleagues of the time. It is likely that not all of this stemmed from a natural, spontaneous, almost physiological handling of the Beatles myth.

The history of popular publishing and consumption, in fact, tells us that the comic strip was seen at the dawn of its mass distribution (in the thirties, across the Atlantic) as a symptom if not of rebellion then at least of something alternative, capable of taking the place of the quiet life, of the placid images of the time. And this, thanks to instinct, to good fortune and to a state of grace to which The Beatles bore witness not just artistically, was perhaps a decisive motive, a driving force for their metamorphosis into a comic strip.

Beatlemania itself, with the photos and film strips documenting that frenzy of cheerful and carefree zaniness, seems to be a phenomenon straight out of Duckburg—characters rippling in free motion, with the swarming, ebullient mob of fans that not even kryptonite could have stopped in those years.

And when the magnificent trajectory, that waking dream, began to fall into decline, with breakup and farewell by now just round the corner, the features of the paper heroes would take the place of the exploits of the group. The music is over, and the friends are leaving, each going his or her own way. Free from controversy, from the spiteful words of ordinary people, from diatribes between lawyers and managers, the four Beatles, like it or not, would stay together in the comic strips. Prisoners of a greater destiny, stronger than themselves. There, in the often droll, caricatural lines of affectionate affability in which their adventures are framed, The Beatles will survive forever, without a break, with the balloons above them no longer containing the extraordinary refrains that we have all committed to memory, but serving instead as a means of assimilating the shock and digression, onomatopoeia and transgression, of storing every drop of sensuality and of the legend.

If we think about it, a truly unique and extraordinary way: of eluding the grey zone of the ex, of memory however noble, of the revival to meet the demands of the nostalgic. The Beatles have been catapulted into a segment of storytelling without time or nationality. A profound sign and hey presto!… the journey towards glory has begun, with the promise of never coming to an end. This too is the future. The close encounters can continue…

An angel came down from heaven yesterday

P.S. The title of this introduction and the line that closes it are taken from two of Jimi Hendrix's songs: respectively from the end of "Purple Haze" and from the beginning of "Angel." A way of underlining how the connection and the relations between Hendrix and The Beatles were far less vague and incidental than might be thought. In addition to their mutual esteem, there was one episode in particular that created, in the Swinging London of the sixties, creative, psychedelic, colourful, more in a ferment than ever, an unbreakable link between Jimi and the Fab Four. It is June 1967. The first of the month sees the release, with all the commotion due to one of the most fundamental records in history, *Sgt. Pepper's Lonely Hearts Club Band*, The Beatles' masterpiece, and more. For some time it has been announced that three days later, on 4 June, the Jimi Hendrix Experience will be staging a concert at London's Saville Theatre, run by Brian Epstein, manager of The Beatles: who have all been invited, even though no one knows who is going to turn up on the night. At the beginning of the show Paul McCartney and George Harrison are present. They know Jimi's music well and appreciate it, though up until that moment just one LP, *Are You Experienced?*, and a couple of singles have come out. In a *coup de théâtre*, the first number on the bill is a raw and passionate version of the track "Sgt. Pepper's Lonely Hearts Club Band," turned on its head and transformed by Hendrix's genius—practically an instant cover that a long time afterwards Paul, in his autobiography *Many Years from Now*, will have no hesitation in singling out as "one of the great honours of my career." Perfect, if you think about it, for a comic-strip story…

Sgt. Pepper's in Comics Land

or

The Beatles in Comic Strips: How to Conquer the World and Become Unforgettable

Fabio Schiavo

A subtle thread links The Beatles to comic strips. And not just because the four musicians had always been fanatic readers of those comics printed on cheap paper that looked as if they were going to fall apart from one moment to the next, at the mere touch of a hand. Genuine icons of pop culture, like Marilyn and Coca-Cola, they were fated to meet up with the "most classic means of expression, with a clear *popular* bent," a medium with great narrative and entertainment capacities that easily grabbed the attention of teens of both sexes. But it was the girls who fell most under the spell of John, Paul, George and Ringo. And this could even be the ruin of a young woman torn in her affections, as is recounted in "The Beatles Were My Downfall!," the title of *Summer Love* no. 46 in October 1965; at the same time, though, it could revive flagging love, as in "The Beatles Saved My Romance," again in *Summer Love*, but this time no. 47 of October the following year. In perfect contrast is the semantic irony of *Laugh* no. 166, January 1965, in which the different and antithetical perception of the musical phenomenon on the part of teenagers and their parents is represented in the balloons by simple drawings: in that of the dreamy fans listening to one of the group's records we see images of The Beatles, while in that of the father, who is gazing at them with fury as his reading of the newspaper is disturbed by that "infernal noise," there are four real beetles. Same sound, different meaning, incredibly funny effect. Worthy of slapstick comedy.

It is interesting to note that from 1963, the year of their debut in the world of comics with various appearances in the British magazines for teenage girls *Boyfriend*, *Roxy* and *Valentine*, to our own day, not a single year has passed without the publication of a strip in which Lennon, McCartney, Harrison, Starr and their songs are the protagonists, whether recollected, parodied or at least cited. Whence the observation that the Fab Four have never left Comics Land and the real world, constructing a paper trail, despite the fact they have not existed as a group since 1970, that stretches all the way from the West to Japan.

The Beatles have been described as a global phenomenon with a great impact on the media and on music. Yet no one seems to have been aware of these signs. Except one quite closed, highly Catholic and fairly traditionalistic European country. Apart from the first, predictable and obvious, appearances on the home market in 1963, the only place that realized what was going on in cold and distant Albion was, incredible as it may seem, Spain, certainly no model of openness towards the outside, or of democracy and modernity. The publications, simple photographic reportages, were all in women's magazines, weeklies with unambiguous titles like *Serenata* and *Romántica*, not to mention *Mary Noticias*—a romantic picture story told in drawings that recounts the adventures of a girl reporter and her fiancé—and in any case represent an undoubted first.

The earliest depiction in a proper comic strip, however, is British. In February 1964, *The Dandy*, a weekly comic for children, published an amusing parody based on mice, cats and the citation of one of the quartet's hits, "She Loves You," transformed into "She Loves Cheese." This was followed by more traditional publications in the women's magazines *Diana for Girls*, *Marilyn* and *Valentine*, the first to use the titles of the Fab Four's various hits as the basis for the creation of romantic comic-strip stories turning on the thesis *amor vincit omnia*, a formula also taken up by the Spanish *Claro de Luna* in the same years and that was to endure until the early seventies. Again in 1964, but in Italy, a fairly realistic history of the band, drawn by Enrico Bagnoli, appeared in four parts, one for each member of the group, in the supplement dedicated to young people of the weekly *ABC*, an Italian magazine that mixed politics and *risqué* reports. Cool! Or rather, fab!

In America, the meeting between The Beatles and comic strips would prove advantageous to both. To the quartet it would open the doors of success, while to the comics it would offer new life after a period of near annihilation due to the publication, in 1954, of *Seduction of the Innocent*, a book by the psychiatrist Fredric Wertham in which the author claimed that comic books had a negative effect on the development of the young and that there was a link between them and drugs, sex, violence and delinquency. The book, which came out in a period that had also seen Senator Joseph McCarthy's crusade against the communist threat, led to a series of hearings of the author before members of the Congress to explain the phenomenon and the consequent adoption of a self-regulatory code for the sector. And so at the moment of the "British invasion"—as the arrival in the US of various British bands in the wake of The Beatles' success would be defined by American newspapers of the time—the country did not find itself unprepared, marshalling an incredible amount of firepower. And varied too: ranging from the mockery of *Sick* and *Mad* to the irony of *Archie* and comprising the sentimentality of *My Little Margie*, with a pining little girl on the cover. And then there were no. 130 of *Strange Tales* with the headline "How Off-Beat Can You Get? Don't Dare Miss the Human Torch and the Ever-Lovin' Blue-Eyed Thing When They… 'Meet… The Beatles!'", with Ben Grimm and Johnny Storm given a pageboy haircut, and *Superman's Pal, Jimmy Olsen* no. 79, where he is transformed into "The Red-Headed Beatle of 1,000 B.C.!" and transported to an imaginary past, triggering a real Beatle craze complete with appropriate merchandising. Nor should we forget Dell Comic's exceptional *Complete Life Stories*, recounting the life of the four Beatles from childhood until their arrival in America, with our heroes turned into American college boys wearing penny loafers on their feet.

Endowed with charismatic personalities, The Beatles—who were to become the most important media phenomena of the last century and a subject of sociological analysis—evoked an incredible "collective imagery," one of "evolutionary agents sent by God, endowed with

a mysterious power to create a new human species" (as Timothy Leary put it), making themselves the voices of a globalized world of youth ahead of its time. Simultaneously, they were turned into perfect marketing creations, capable of selling anything, from wigs—incredible the story that appeared in *Betty & Veronica* no. 105, of which an extract is published on page 27— to picnic hampers, bars of soap to chewing gum, and even wallpaper and window curtains; in short real money-making machines. All it took was their name and Bob's your uncle! As is demonstrated by the advertisement in *Love Diary*, July 1965, for Beatle mops to grow at home ("watch them grow their own hair live in your own room"), a para-trichological version of the famous "Sea-Monkeys" on sale by mail-order in various comic books in the decade 1960–70. Not bad for long-haired adolescents seen as no more than a band for teenagers, and certainly not destined to last for long. The Beatles, however, had other plans: to become "the toppermost of the poppermost" and "more famous than Elvis Presley," and, above all, to have fun. Within a few years they had done this and much more, to the point of being able to claim they were "more popular than Jesus," triggering hysteria and the burning of their records and books and magazines about them. Emerging unscathed, they went on to become fashion leaders, to be regarded as emissaries of Satan and even to rise to the status of a musical myth; receiving, in the meantime, death threats from the Ku Klux Klan, an event recorded in *Honkytonk Sue*, a comic strip created by Bob Boze Bell and published in 1980 that turned them into kings of Country and Western.
As for The Beatles as Trojan horse of the Dark Lord, willing servants of his plan to subject the free world to his evil will, the tenth issue of the Christian comic *The Crusaders*, entitled "Spellbound?," revives the theories put forward by the Reverend David A. Noebel in congenial pamphlets like *Communism, hypnotism and the Beatles* and *The Beatles: A Study in Drugs, Sex, & Revolution*. The comic book, brought out by Chick Publications, stressed that black magic, the subliminal messages that wicked rock musicians hide between the grooves of their discs, the celebration of strange and foreign rituals, the glorification of libertine and licentious sexual behaviour, and even too much democracy and lack of respect for necessary differences and above all of regard for the Word of God are the clearest signs of the continual and mounting conspiracy against the wholesome American Way of Life, an operation conducted by Powers of Darkness and Mysterious Alliances that hate the Land of Freedom and its youth wholly devoted to motherhood and apple pie. N.B. Among the numerous sworn enemies of Mr Jack Thomas Chick, the creator of the publications, we find: Freemasons, Muslims, Roman Catholics and the pope, Communists, politicians in general, Harry Potter, New Age and pop culture, to name just a few. It goes without saying that he is certainly not a supporter of Darwin's theory of evolution and considers premarital sex, abortion and homosexuality *very* bad things.

Even though it all looked as if it would last forever in those years of easy living for the publishing industry, the first rumours had begun to circulate about the possible end of the group. And so the creators of stories were seized by doubt. So long as The Beatles existed as a unit, bringing out comic books about them made sense, but if they were to break up? What would happen then? The answer was not slow in coming. Absolutely NOTHING. Everything went on just like before. In fact, the band's breakup has not meant the end of such publications. Indeed, quite the opposite.

It could even be argued that, proportionally, they have increased. They range from citations of science fiction in Mike Allred's *Red Rocket 7* or Antonio Serra's *Gregory Hunter* and *Nathan Never*, published by Bonelli, to the transformation of The Beatles into aliens, or rather Skrulls, in the Pete Wisdom series and Paul Cornell's *Captain Britain and MI:13*; from the magical ravings of Alan Moore in *Promethea* to the Ringo revenant of the eclectic Rob Zombie, aka Robert Bartleh Cummings, in *El Superbeasto*; from the iconoclasm of *National Lampoon* to that of the Simpsons; intersecting with the Italian comics published under the Disney imprint: in 1993 *Topolino e il quarto Beatle* ("Mickey Mouse and the Fourth Beatle") by Bruno Sarda and Andrea Ferraris and in 2008 *La canzone fuori tempo* ("The Timeless Song") by Giorgio Salati and Paolo Mottura. In the middle we find the kidnapping of our lads foiled by a South-American Indian superhero in *Las grandes andanzas de Patoruzú e Isidoro* by Dante Quinterno, the sexy encounter with the most famous paper pin-up in the world and regular guest in *Playboy*, Little Annie Fanny, the lunacies of the American satirical magazine *Mad*—don't miss the back cover with Ringo endorsing a shampoo made of bleach in a mock advert drawn by Frank Frazetta—and much more.

And then, again, the strips created in 1966 by Gion, singer and bass guitarist of I Balordi, published in Italy in the music weekly *Ciao Amici*; the four, in pirate dress, who in *Alika* no. 14, entitled "Aiuto! i Beatles" ("Help! The Beatles"), meet the eponymous space heroine, Claudio Villa and the Italian comic character Pappagone; the strip-cartoon versions of the film *Yellow Submarine*; the Mexican delirium of Rafael Araiza's *Las Comadres*, 1968, where the transplant of a young girl's heart into a super macho man transforms him into a frenzied and adoring fan of the Fab Four.

What to say then of the detective story *Mersey Sound*, drawn by Grassilli for *Alter*, of the citations in Quino's *Mafalda*, of the malice shown by the youngsters in *Il Male* on the occasion of Lennon's death, of the anarchic *El hombre de los caramelos*, a graphic folly made in Spain, and of the reinterpretation of Manara in *Storie brevi* with the tale *John Lennon*, where the deceased musician arrives in heaven and sings one of Macca's songs, "Sgt. Pepper's Lonely Hearts Club Band," waking up a place that seemed to have fallen asleep and to be peopled by nothing but divine images and representations. Imagine there's no heaven...

Let's go!

1960—1970

Strange paradoxes. As early as 1963, in Spain at the height of the Francoist regime, the magazines for *muchachas*, i.e. with a readership of teenage girls, spoke without any hesitation or censorship about a wannabe famous group of mop-headed English musicians and their songs. Four years later, in Greece, a similar regime, that of the "Colonels," known as the

TELL ME WHY

Junta (η Χούντα), in power from 1967 to 1974, put a ban on The Beatles as soon as they had carried out their *coup d'état*, along with "long hair, miniskirts, Sophocles, Tolstoy, Mark Twain, Euripides" and many other things, including "modern music, pop music, modern mathematics, peace movements and the letter Z, which means 'he lives' in ancient Greek."

the Beatles 1960–1970

1960

17 August. A group of young musicians from Liverpool, The Silver Beatles, arrives in Hamburg, to play in various clubs in the city.

1961

21 February. With their new and definitive name, The Beatles make their debut at the Cavern, an important club in their native city. In August, returning to Germany for more concerts in Hamburg, they release a single, "My Bonnie," on which they are accompanied by the singer Tony Sheridan.

9 November. Brian Epstein, their future manager, hears The Beatles for the first time, at the Cavern Club, where their fame is growing.

1962

24 January. After an unsuccessful audition for Decca, Epstein reaches an agreement with The Beatles to manage them and guide their work.

8 March. The Beatles make their first radio appearance, on the BBC.

4 June. The Beatles sign contracts with EMI and two days later are in the Abbey Road Studios, making a recording under the direction of George Martin. Four tracks are laid down, a cover of "Bésame mucho" and their own compositions "P.S. I Love You," "Ask Me Why" and "Love Me Do."

18 August. Ringo Starr, the drummer of another local band, Rory Storm & The Hurricanes, replaces Pete Best and makes his live debut with The Beatles.

5 October. The first single, "Love Me Do," comes out.

28 October. Concert at the Liverpool Empire as a supporting act for Little Richard.

1963

13 January. First appearance on national television, playing "Please Please Me."

2 February. The first British tour starts in Bradford, Yorkshire: they are paid 80 pounds a week, to be divided in four.

4 May. The single "From Me to You" reaches the top of the charts (where it will stay for seven weeks, selling over 650,000 copies).

11 May. Same success for the debut album, called *Please Please Me*, with fourteen songs, eight of them written by Lennon and McCartney.

1 August. The first issue of the magazine *Beatles Monthly* comes out: it will be published until December '69, with 77 issues and a peak circulation of 350,000 copies.

3 August. Last of 274 performances at the Cavern Club.

13 October. After scenes of hysteria at the concert at the Palladium in London the term "Beatlemania" is coined.

14 December. "I Want to Hold Your Hand" is number one in the singles charts: advance sales alone total 940,000 copies.

1964

7 February. The Beatles land in New York for their first visit to the US. It is estimated that their TV performance of the 9th, on *The Ed Sullivan Show*, is watched by 73 million viewers. On the 11th, live debut at Washington Coliseum.

15 February. *Meet The Beatles!* is the best-selling album in the United States.

28 March. Statues of The Beatles are put up in Madame Tussauds wax museum in London.

4 April. Five Beatles singles occupy the top five positions on the Billboard charts: "Can't Buy Me Love," "Twist and Shout," "She Loves You," "I Want to Hold Your Hand" and "Please Please Me."

23 May. Ella Fitzgerald is the first artist to get into charts with a cover of The Beatles, "Can't Buy Me Love."

4 June. The first world tour starts at K. B. Hallen in Copenhagen.

6 July. World première of the film *A Hard Day's Night*, directed by Richard Lester, at the Pavilion Theatre in London.

20 August. Their fee for a performance at the Municipal Stadium in Kansas City on the second American tour shatters the world record: 150,000 dollars.

2 December. Ringo undergoes an operation on his tonsils at a hospital in London.

1965

23 February. Shooting of The Beatles' second film starts in Nassau, Bahamas: the director is Lester again.

13 April. The Beatles win two Grammy Awards.

7 June. Last radio session for the BBC. By the end of the month The Beatles will be in Milan, Genoa and Rome for their only tour of Italy: the feat of arranging the tour is pulled off by the impresario Leo Wachter.

11 August. World première of the film *Help!*: seven new songs are included in the soundtrack.

15 August. Record takings for the concert at the Shea Stadium in New York, with 304,000 dollars and 55,600 spectators.

25 September. The series of animated cartoons *The Beatles* makes its debut on the American TV channel ABC, with episodes lasting half an hour each.

9 October. "Yesterday," the song by The Beatles that today boasts the largest number of cover versions—in the thousands—is at number one in the US charts.

3 December. *Rubber Soul* comes out: the album, which enjoys enormous success, is hailed for its innovative quality and many great songs.

1966

21 January. George Harrison marries Patti Boyd, whom he met on the set of *A Hard Day's Night*: Paul McCartney is best man.

1 May. The group's last British appearance at the Empire Pool in Wembley, for the annual New Musical Express Poll Winners Concert.

30 June. First of three concerts at the Budokan in Tokyo.

30 July. The album *"Yesterday"... and Today* reaches number one on the US charts. It will go down in history for its "butcher cover," whose gruesome images lead to the recall of the record. The original will become much sought after by collectors.

20 August. The single "Yellow Submarine" sung by Ringo Starr is number one in Great Britain. "Eleanor Rigby" is on the B-side.

29 August. The last concert, at Candlestick Park in San Francisco: the song that marks the end of the line for their live career is Little Richard's "Long Tall Sally."

9 November. John Lennon meets Yoko Ono at the Indica Gallery in London during the preview of her exhibition *Unfinished Paintings and Objects*.

26 November. The recording sessions for the next album begin at the Abbey Road Studios.

18 December. Screening in London of the film *The Family Way*, for which Paul McCartney has written the soundtrack.

1967

10 February. "A Day in the Life" is recorded: it is the first time that an orchestra with forty players has been used in the history of pop and rock music.

2 March. At the Grammy Awards ceremony, The Beatles win the award for the Song of the Year ("Michelle"), for the Best Contemporary R&R Recording ("Eleanor Rigby") and for the Best Album Cover (*Revolver*).

30 March. Photo-session in a Chelsea studio to create the most famous album cover in history: the packaging of *Sgt. Pepper's Lonely Hearts Club Band* is designed by Pop artist Peter Blake using photographs by Michael Cooper.

18 May. EMI has just announced that sales of Beatles records in the world have exceeded 200 million copies, and Lennon and McCartney do the backing vocals for The Rolling Stones "We Love You."

1 June. *Sgt. Pepper* is in the shops and goes straight to number one in the charts. Staggering figures are being bandied about, from the cost (25,000 pounds) to the hours of work (700).

25 June. "All You Need Is Love" is performed on the first live global television link, to an estimated audience of 400 million viewers: friends and colleagues like Jagger, Richards, Clapton, Keith Moon, Graham Nash and Marianne Faithfull add their voices to the song.

24 July. The four Beatles and Epstein, along with artists, writers and intellectuals, sign a petition for the legalization of marijuana published in *The Times*.

27 August. Brian Epstein, according to *The New York Times* "the man who revolutionized pop music in our time," is found dead in his London home: the cause is an overdose of sleeping pills, following a period of depression.

11 September. Work starts on shooting the TV film *Magical Mystery Tour*, which will be broadcast by the BBC on 26 December. Apple Corps, a multi-armed company that will look after The Beatles' interests and business, is officially founded.

18 October. All the members of the group attend the première in London of the film *How I Won the War*, in which John Lennon plays a leading role.

1 December. Ringo sets off for Rome, where he will act in the film *Candy* shot at Cinecittà.

7 December. The Apple Boutique opens at 94 Baker Street.

1968

7 January. George Harrison composes the music of the film *Wonderwall*, which will be shown at the Cannes Festival on 14 May. The record, on which Harrison plays no instruments, will not come out until November.

25 January. The cameos for the forthcoming animated film *Yellow Submarine* are prepared at Twickenham Film Studios: première in London on 17 July, in the presence of the whole group.

1 February. The Beatles begin their trip to India, heading with families and friends for Rishikesh, the headquarters of Maharishi Mahesh Yogi with whom they will study transcendental meditation. John and George are the first to set off, and are joined later by Paul and Ringo. Ringo will stay only a short time.

9 March. They receive four Grammy Awards for *Sgt. Pepper*.

20 April. Apple Records publishes an advertisement in the newspapers to recruit unknown artists: the discs brought out include recordings by Badfinger, James Taylor, Mary Hopkins, Jackie Lomax, Steve Miller, Billy Preston, Yoko Ono, Ravi Shankar...

26 August. The single "Hey Jude/Revolution" comes out in the US, four days ahead of its release in Great Britain: it is the first 45 on the Apple label. Lasting over seven minutes, it will be the longest song (written by Paul for John's son Julian) to top the charts.

30 September. Hunter Davies authorized biography, *The Beatles*, is published.

22 November. The double LP *The Beatles*, also known as *The White Album*, comes out: in just a few days it sells 2 million copies in the United States alone. It is preceded by about ten days by *Two Virgins*, the experimental and controversial work by John and Yoko.

1969

30 January. The Beatles perform for 42 minutes on the roof of the Apple building, on Savile Row. Takes of the performance will be used for the film *Let It Be*. Billy Preston is on the organ.

12 March. Paul marries Linda Eastman in London.

20 March. Marriage (his second) for John too, who weds Yoko Ono at the British consulate in Gibraltar.

31 March. George and Patti are fined 250 pounds for possession of marijuana (found on them on the day of Paul's wedding).

14 June. "The Ballad of John and Yoko," made by Lennon and McCartney alone, is The Beatles' first stereo single and their last number one in Britain.

8 August. This is the day of the famous photo taken on the zebra crossing in front of the Abbey Road Studios.

20 August. Last recording session of the whole group, to finish "I Want You."

23 August. An article in the *Northern Star*, the daily newspaper of Northern Illinois University, puts forward the hypothesis that Paul had been killed in a car accident on 9 November 1966. It is the beginning of an enduring urban legend.

October-November. *Abbey Road* tops the US and UK LP charts, staying at number one in both countries for eleven weeks.

6 December. "Something," the first single not to bear the signature of Lennon and McCartney, is also a great hit: it is written by George Harrison, and Frank Sinatra calls it the greatest love song of the past fifty years.

1970

11 February. New York première of the film *Magic Christian*, starring Ringo Starr and Peter Sellers.

23 March. The celebrated producer Phil Spector is asked to remix the song "Let It Be," whose sound is considered too dark and not commercial enough. McCartney is not happy with the result and will never be able to stomach it.

9 April. Practically simultaneously with the release of "Let It Be," Paul brings out his debut solo album, *McCartney*, underlining the now irreparable split with the other Beatles. In the meantime John intensifies his work with the Plastic Ono Band and Ringo's *Sentimental Journey* is ready.

13 May. American première, in New York, of the film *Let It Be*. It is premièred a week later in London and Liverpool. The album of the same name soars in the charts, with advance sales alone of 3,700,000 copies.

December. Delayed in its distribution by a transport strike, George Harrison's triple album *All Things Must Pass* comes out.

30 December. Paul McCartney launches legal proceedings to dissolve his contractual ties with the other Beatles.

THE BEATLE BROWSE

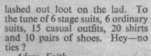

Starting now. The weekly column by the Merseyside sensations The Beatles. This page is strictly from them to you. News and discs with facts about the fabulous four fellas who have cracked the British Top Twenty wide open.

W... think... and a... John... Over t...

DOW...

THINGS... wise... that it's t... Mersey mo... ten scene ne... with a great... *The Big Thre*... Hutchinson (drums/vocals); Johnny Gustafson (bass guitar/vocals); and Brian Griffiths (lead guitar/vocals). Mighty few frills about this lot—hard driving punchy rocking beat

...ing else ...u don't ...t braid ...bance) ...cene.

...dance craze, ...*Stomp*. Equipment required: One copy of The Big Three's disc, a solid floor, massive muscles and a towel—for drying off afterwards.

(*J.L. Back to the kennel, Harrison, while Ringo Starr uncorks the Beatlebottle*).

🍾 BEATLEBOTTLE OF POP

THE bottle's blowin' its cork, so let's get Genie on the job. What's new, big G?

It's Genie for Gene for a start off Ringo—Gene Pitney. Things have been thin for Gene hitwise since Gonna Love My Life Away. *But he's on a good thing with* True Love Never Runs Smooth (*United Artists*). *Well worth your spintime.*

I'll give it a whirl. Next please? *Can't go wrong with the Four Seasons. All the usual gimmicks on* Marlena *backed with* Candy Girl (*Stateside*). *Another winner.* Well done Genie—back to the bottle, slave!

(*J.L. That's all from you. Now over to Paul McCartney with the Beatle Buzz*).

BEATLE BUZZ

BIG deal for *Joe Brown*. A shoemaking firm with branches all over the country are

to produce the Joe Brown boot. Joe had a hand—if you can have a hand in a boot—in designing

the new footwear. Roughly it's a half boot, but the uppers look like an old fashioned spat. Looking at the first model, Joe saw that the uppers fastened with a single mother of pearl button. "Change that to a bone button," ordered Joe. The firm asked why. "Too flash," says Joe.

Danny Williams has a new sports car which he's had super charged to make it go faster. He's also had a record player built into the sports car and bought an American LP called *Music To Speed By*!

First singer to be promoted by Larry Parnes for four years— 18 year old *Daryl Quist* from Canada. That's his *real* name, too. Larry—who started *Tommy Steele, Billy Fury, Marty Wilde* and others— swore he had given up finding talent, but he reckons Daryl could be the greatest. As proof he has

lashed out loot on the lad. To the tune of 6 stage suits, 6 ordinary suits, 15 casual outfits, 20 shirts and 10 pairs of shoes. Hey—no ties?

Adam Faith will play the starring role in a stage production of *Tom Sawyer* which will open in a West End theatre later this year.

After fierce argument, *The Tornados* staged a go-kart race at Great Yarmouth, refereed by *Mark Wynter, Joe Brown* and *Rolf Harris. Clem Cattini* rolls up first and gets the fastest kart. So he's round the first bend while the others are still getting started. But, led by *Alan Caddy*, the lads left the track and cut across country. So when Clem belts up to the winning post they're all waiting to cheer him home. Where were the referees? Doubled up laughing.

Still getting over the shock of their first trip to the Smoke (London) are *Johnny Hudson and the Teenbeats*, Scotland's most popular group. Travelling down in their wagon for a Decca recording date, they arrived too late to book in anywhere. So they parked on Hampstead Heath. Waking all bleary-eyed at dawn they found themselves next to some fairground folk—who heard their story with sympathy. In next to no time they were fixed up with a portable shower bath, breakfast and lots of tea. They thanked their new friends who said that was okay—and charged the lads 15/- each! Hope that fair never visits Scotland.

So it's John Lennon *saying cheerio till next week when once again we'll make our Beatlebow. Till then!*

First picture ever published of our office. You can't see the padded walls or the window bars but you'll notice all the other office furniture is there.

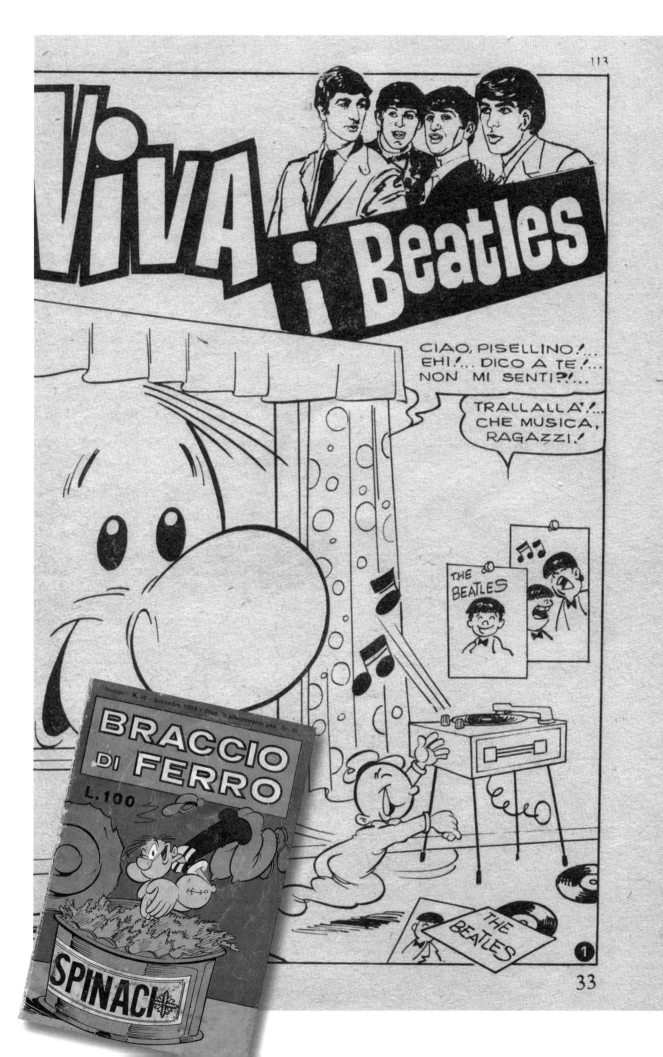

ACROSS THE UNIVERSE

Sexy, provocative and uninhibited, Alika is the heroine of the fortnightly science-fiction comic book which was brought out in 1965 and only lasted for twenty issues. No. 12, *Il cavaliere mascherato*, was taken out of circulation by the censors and no. 21 was announced but never published. If Barbarella, a similar character of those years, is the unfaithful woman of space, Alika, an intergalactic Venus from the planet Absur, "has a licence to love." The stories, in the early issues, are in science-fiction/sexy key, while the later ones are in a more satirical vein. As in no. 14, "Aiuto! i Beatles" ("Help! The Beatles"), drawn by Angelo Todaro, *nom de plume* Paul Bennet, and alluding to the Italian title of the Fab Four's film *Help!*. The adventure with vaguely conservative tones is a surreal psychedelic pastiche that blends Dumas and modernity, transforming The Beatles into *Scarafaggettieri* (a play on the Italian name for the musketeers, *moschettieri*, incorporating the Italian word for beetle, *scarafaggio*), antagonists of the pirate Claudio Villa and Pappagone, mixing swashbuckling romance in the style of Angelica with the first hints of a veiled—very veiled—eroticism.

Condorito • no. 13 • Cover Pepo • Zig Zag Empresa Editorial S.A. • Chile • **1964**

HUGGABLE to Knit LOVABLE BEAT DOLLS!

Want to get your hands on those fab Beat boys? Well, just get clicking with your knitting needles and you'll have four doll-sized darlings to hug to your heart! The full, easy-to-follow instructions are FREE to all readers of MIRABELLE—you'll find details of how to send for them below.

For your free copy of the Beat Doll Instructions, cut out the coupon below and send it together with a stamped, self-addressed envelope to: "Beat Dolls," MIRABELLE, Tower House, Southampton Street, London, W.C.2.

MIRABELLE Beat Doll Coupon

10

MIRABELLE Charm Club

PATSY LEARNS some Charm Club tricks on MAKING EYES!

RINGO on our back cover. No. 2 of our SUPER SOLO BEATLES!

Mirabelle 6D
Romance and Pops for Every Girl!

FREE! INSIDE SIX SUPER COLOUR PORTRAIT STAMPS

MAKE THEM! HUG THEM! BEAT DOLLS!

JUST ARRIVED! CLIFF! FIRST colour portrait from his new film

Frankie's girl
The tender story of a Coffee-Bar romance.

1964 • Mirabelle • no. 2 • C. Arthur Pearson Ltd • United Kingdom

Diana for Girls • no. 65 • D. C. Thomson & Co Ltd, John Leng & Co Ltd •

THOR IS MY GUIDE DOG, I CAN'T GO ANYWHERE WITHOUT HIM. HE'S SO BIG HE NEEDS A SEAT FOR HIMSELF!

OH, I'M SORRY! I DIDN'T NOTICE.

It hurt Yvonne to say what she did about her favourite pop stars.

At long last we reached the booking office, and the precious ticket was in my hands.

YOU TWO LADIES ARE CERTAINLY LUCKY. YOU'VE GOT THE LAST TWO TICKETS!

THE LAST TWO! HOW SUPER!

I'M AFRAID THAT TICKET ISN'T ANY USE TO ME—UNLESS I CAN TAKE MY GUIDE DOG IN WITHOUT A TICKET.

IF ONLY I COULD HELP. SHE'S SO DISAPPOINTED!

WELL, IF THIS WERE JUST AN ORDINARY CONCERT THAT WOULD BE ALLOWED—BUT NOT IN THIS CASE. YOU'LL NEED A TICKET FOR THE DOG, I'M SORRY.

HERE, PLEASE TAKE MY TICKET FOR YOUR DOG! I DON'T LIKE THE BEATLES VERY MUCH ANYWAY!

THANK YOU! I'LL NEVER BE AB...

Back home, I went up to my room, I couldn't help feeling sorry for myself.

I DID SO WANT TO SEE THE BEATLES. I'LL JUST HAVE TO BE CONTENT TO WATCH THEM ON T.V.

On Saturday, the day of the concert, my brothers set off for the Town Hall.

WE'LL BRING YOU BACK A PROGRAMME, YVONNE!

LOOK OUT FOR US ON TELEVISION!

ENJOY YOURSELVES, AND GIVE MY LOVE TO THE BEATLES.

AS A MATTER OF FACT, YVONNE, I HEARD HOW YOU GAVE UP YOUR TICKET FOR A BLIND GIRL'S DOG. THE LITTLE GIRL WAS IN MY SHOP TODAY. WHY DON'T YOU COME ALONG WITH ME? I COULD DO WITH AN ASSISTANT.

But...

...round at once. He shook his head when he examined the set.

...S. THE SET NEEDS ...ND I WON'T BE ...RKING TONIGHT.

...H! THAT MEANS I WON'T SEE THE BEATLES!

Before I knew what w... in the electrician's van... where I was...

WHERE ARE WE GOING ...IT HAVE BEEN BETTE... ...THE CROWDS IN THE SQUARE?

WE'VE GOT TO GO THROUGH HERE TO GET TO THE TOWN HALL. WE'RE HELPING WITH THE LIGHTS FOR THE SECOND SHOW TONIGHT!

I wasn't much help with the lights, I'm afraid. I was too busy watching my idols from the wings. Ringo, George, Paul and John—they were so near, I could almost have reached out and touched them! And down near the front of the audience I could see Thor the Alsatian sitting, head erect and ears cocked. I'm sure his tail was keeping time to the fab music. It certainly was the most wonderful evening of my life!

DIANA for GIRLS

No. 65—16th MAY 1964
EVERY MONDAY - 6d.

Great Complete Story Inside
"How Yvonne Met The Beatles"

8

DELL
GIANT
35c

07-059-411

SEPT.—NOV.

THE BEATLES

OFFICIAL

COMPLETE LIFE STORIES

8 PIN-UP PICTURES

COLOR PHOTOS

♥ GEORGE HARRISON
♥ JOHN LENNON
♥ PAUL McCARTNEY
♥ RINGO STARR

© 1964 NEMS
ENTERPRISES, LTD.

Mad • no. 90 • E. C. Publications • USA • 1964

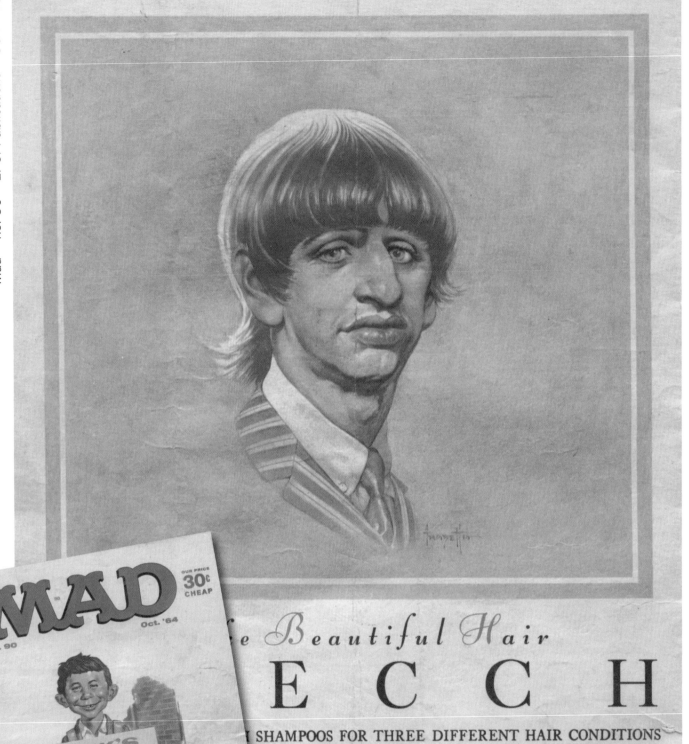

For The Beautiful Hair

BLECCH

3 SHAMPOOS FOR THREE DIFFERENT HAIR CONDITIONS

• For dry hair—a special formula that takes neat crew-cut type hair and lays it down over your ears. • For oily hair—loosens up that slick-combing stuff so it spills down over your eyes. • For normal hair—gives it proper body so it mushrooms all over your head. Get the shampoo that's right for you, and make your hair "Blecch"! Yeah! Yeah! Yeah!

BLECCH SHAMPOO D For Dry Hair
BLECCH SHAMPOO O For Oily Hair
BLECCH SHAMPOO N For Normal Hair

MAD
OUR PRICE 30¢ CHEAP
Oct. '64
NO. 90

FINK'S
DONUTS

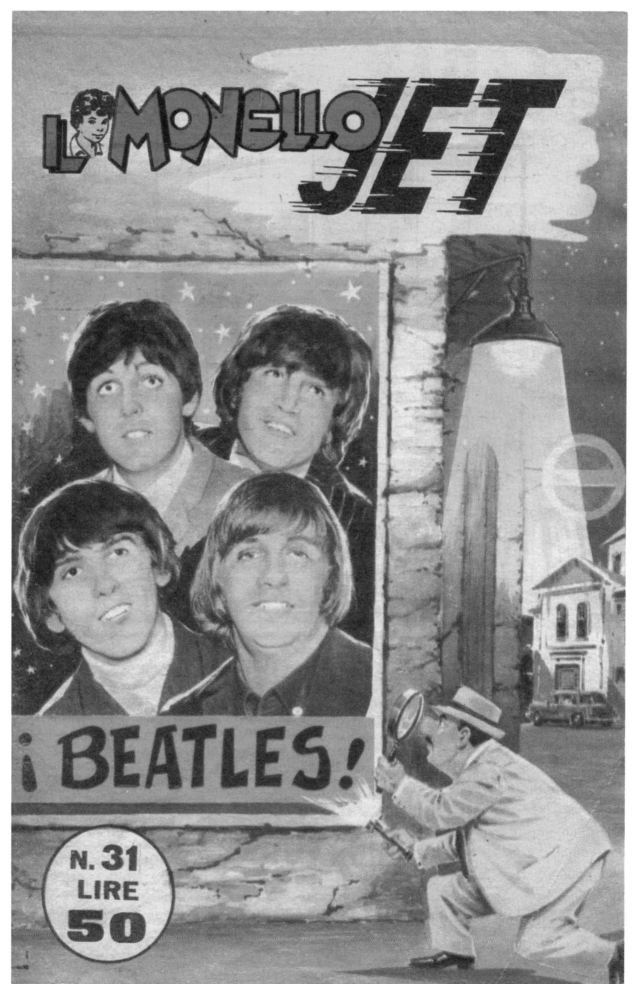

Tintin • no. 855 • Dargaud S.A. Editeur • France • 1965

N° 855
17ᵉ ANNÉE
11 MARS 1965

HEBDOMADAIRE
Fr. 1
Prix en Suisse : 1 fr. S
Prix en Algérie : 115 Frs

TINTIN

LE JOURNAL DES JEUNES DE 7 A 77 ANS

Dans ce numéro :
Le CROSS « TINTIN »,
UN CONCOURS PASSIONNANT !

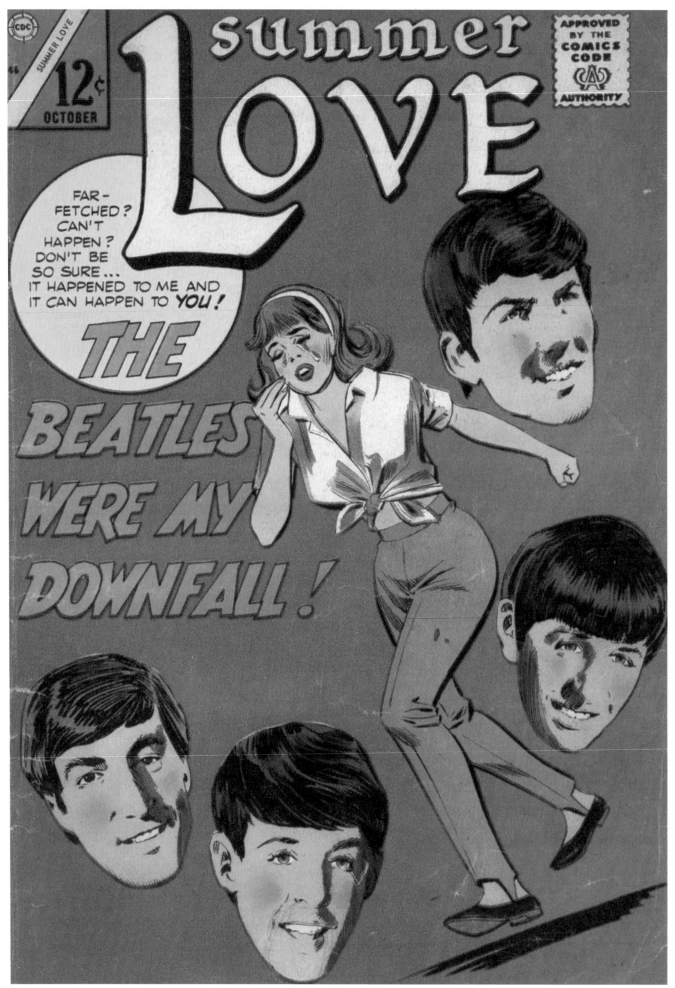

1966 • Teddy Bob • no. 2 • Editrice C.E.A. • Italy

Big Daddy Roth • no. 2 • Millar Publishing Company • USA • 1966

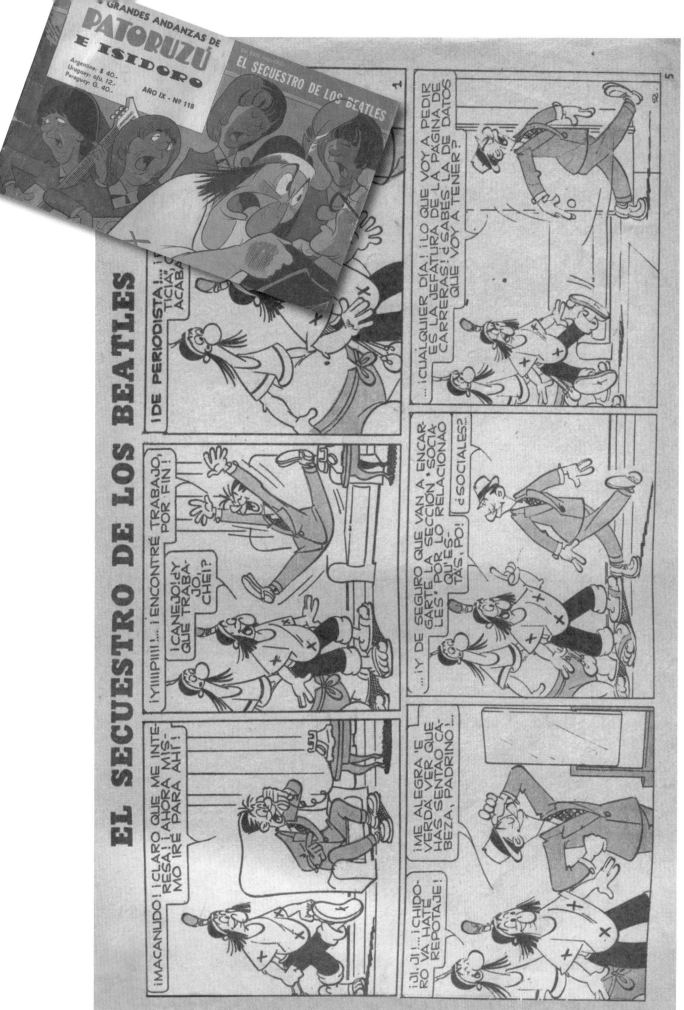

DO YOU WANT TO KNOW A SECRET?

In Spain the comic is called *tebeo*. The name derives from *TBO*, one of the earliest publications in the genre. The best-known magazines for teenage girls were *Rosas Blancas, Mary Noticias, Serenata, Romántica* and *Claro de Luna*. Among those who worked on the latter, founded in 1959, were Enric Badía Romero (*Modesty Blaise* and *Rahan*), Miguel Gómez Esteban (*Gringo, Dossier Negro, Vampirella*), and Carme Barbará Geniés. The mixed-gender editorial staff, one of the first in the sector, was an innovation for the time and the country. The weekly, published by Ibero Mundial de Ediciones, offered "news, information and photographs" on "actors, singers and favourites of the female public" and used the inside and outside back cover for "portraits of groups, singers or fashionable figures," without forgetting the love stories in comic strips that were based on the titles of hit songs. In the six hundred issues of *Claro de Luna* brought out in over ten years, The Beatles appeared a total of 35 times.

Punch • Bradbury Agnew & Co Ltd • Odhams Press Ltd • United Kingdom • 1966

PUNCH 23 NOVEMBER 1966
ONE SHILLING & SIXPENCE

A BEATLE talks to Patrick Catling

1967 • Smash! A Power Comic • no. 94 • Odhams Press Ltd • United Kingdom

THE MAN FROM B.U.N.G.L.E.

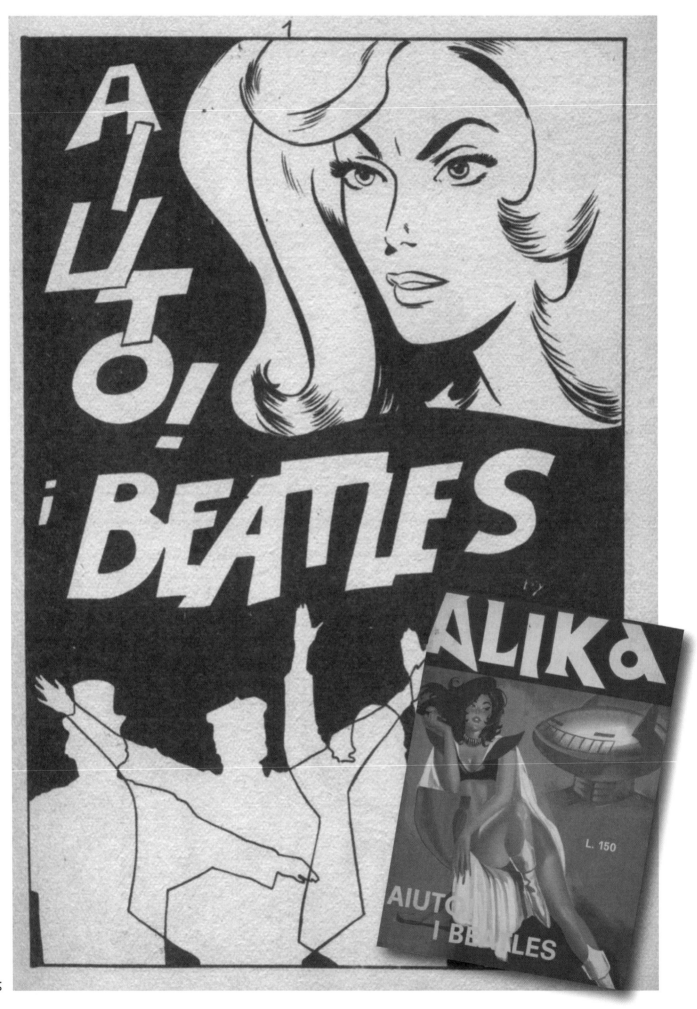

17

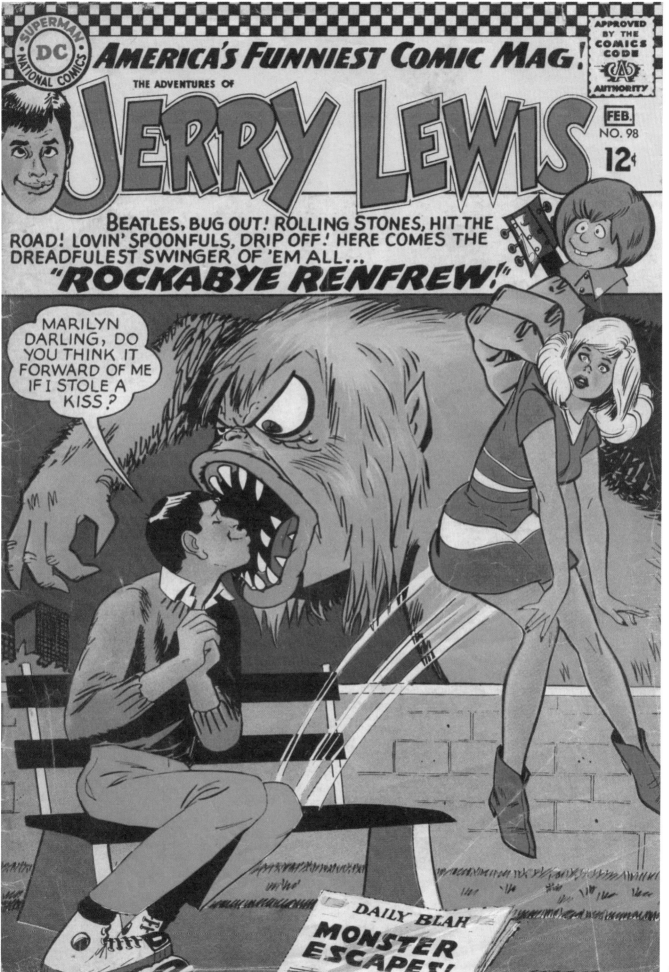

¿VES, MAMA? ¿VES COMO AHORA ME SALE?

¡SEÑOR JOHN LENNON! ¿QUÉ SE HA CREIDO USTED? ¡VENGA, ESE BANJO! ¡NUNCA ESPERE DISGUSTO SEMEJANTE!

"TEMBLOR ANTICIPADO EN EL TRASERO DE JOHN LENNON. ¡AHORA VENDRÁ EL SUPERCASTIGO PEDIDO POR EL PROFE!

¿PARA ESO ME PASO HORAS ENSEÑÁNDOTE? EL "SAINT LOUIS BLUES" ES ASÍ, NO COMO TÚ LO TOCAS.

"QUEDA JUGADO EL DESTINO DE JOHN LENNON. SI SU MADRE FUERA UNA MADRE COMÚN, INDIGNADA PALIZA ENROJECERÍA EL TRASERO DE JOHN, Y VAYA UNO A SABER A QUE ALCANTARILLA DE LA CONCIENCIA IRIAN A PARAR SUS INCLINACIONES MUSICALES."

"PERO LA VIDA ES RISA Y ES LAGRIMAS. A LOS CATORCE AÑOS JOHN SUFRE LA MÁS CRUEL DE LAS TRAGEDIAS: PIERDE A LA MADRE. NADIE PUEDE SABERLO. PERO ES POSIBLE QUE EN TANTA TRISTEZA ESTEN NACIENDO LAS CANCIONES MÁS SENTIDAS DEL GRAN COMPOSITOR QUE UN DÍA SERÁ JOHN LENNON.

LOS QUARRYMEN, EL PRIMER CONJUNTO. EN EL AÑO DE GRACIA DE 1953

"LA CASA DE UNA TIA, LA TIA MIMÍ, QUE TAMBIEN ES BUENA, TOLERANTE, JOHN PUEDE SEGUIR DISTRAYENDOSE. LA PELEA ES ENTRE EL ESTUDIO Y LA MÚSICA. IMAGÍNENSE QUIEN GANA. JOHN CONTAGIA A VARIOS COMPAÑEROS, FORMAN UN GRUPO, ENSAYAN CUANTAS VECES PUEDEN ROBARLE TIEMPO A LOS DEBERES DEL COLEGIO, O SEA CASI SIEMPRE. EL NOMBRE DEL GRUPO ES "QUARRYMEN", LO SACAN DEL NOMBRE DEL COLEGIO"

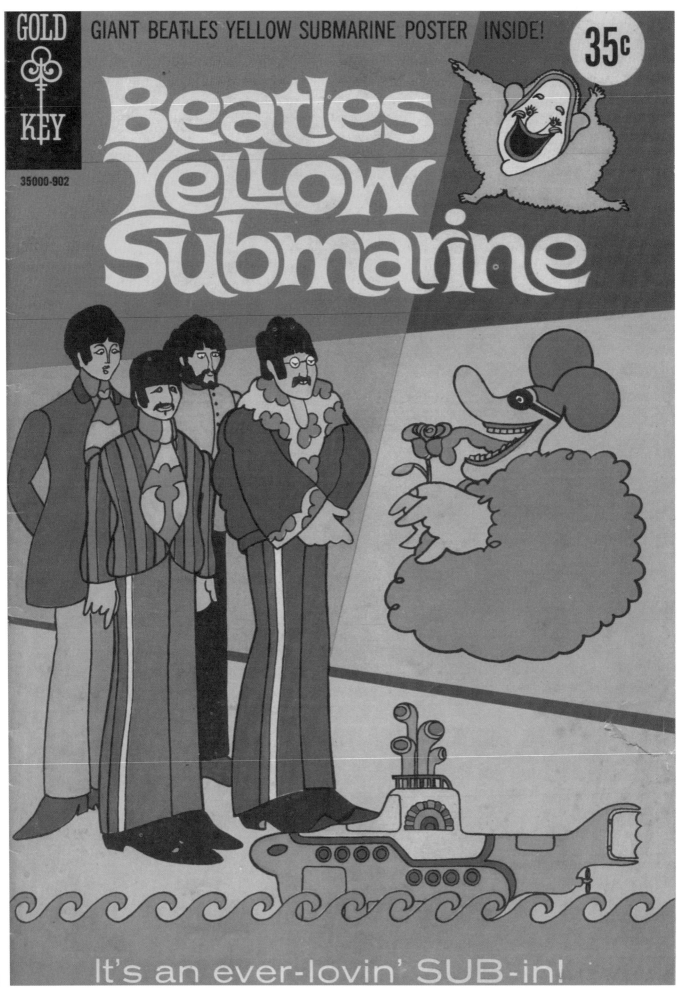

Pepperland är ockuperat av fientliga styrkor. Musikhatande Blånekare har stulit all färg och all glädje. Det finns bara en chans att befria landet. Den gula undervattensbåten startar sin färd genom många farliga hav till ett land långt borta för att hämta De Oöövervinnerliga Beatles.

CRY BABY CRY

The *Historias De Hoy* comic books conceived by Héctor Gérman Oesterheld (Buenos Aires, 23 July 1919 – 21 April 1977), one of the most innovative and interesting Argentine comic-strip writers, were intended as modern cribs introducing young people to the most important figures of the day. The first in the series, printed in 1968 and realized in collaboration with Alberto and Enrique Breccia, was entitled *La Vida del Ché*, i.e. the life of Ernesto "Che" Guevara. The second, published the same year and drawn by Rubén Sosa, but finished by Gianni Dalfiume, was devoted to The Beatles. This *historieta*, the name used in South America for a comic strip, proved a genuine revolution in graphics and narrative style. In fact drawings were mixed with newspaper cuttings and photos, turning the whole into a cut-up that became in turn a true work of Pop art in perfect tune with the times. As with the one devoted to Che, it is very hard to find original copies of this book: when the Argentinian military seized power by a *coup d'état* in 1976 they seized and destroyed the originals of many of Oesterheld's works owing to their supposed "political" content. The artist suffered the same fate. Picked up by an armed squad, he became a *desaparecido*, along with his daughters Beatriz Marta and Diana Irene, the latter six months pregnant. The same thing happened, in November 1977, to his third daughter, Marina, eight months pregnant, whose husband had already vanished. The following month saw the kidnapping and killing, along with her husband, of the fourth daughter, Estrela Inés, who until that moment had survived the *guerra sucia*, the Dirty War, declared by the Argentinian Junta.

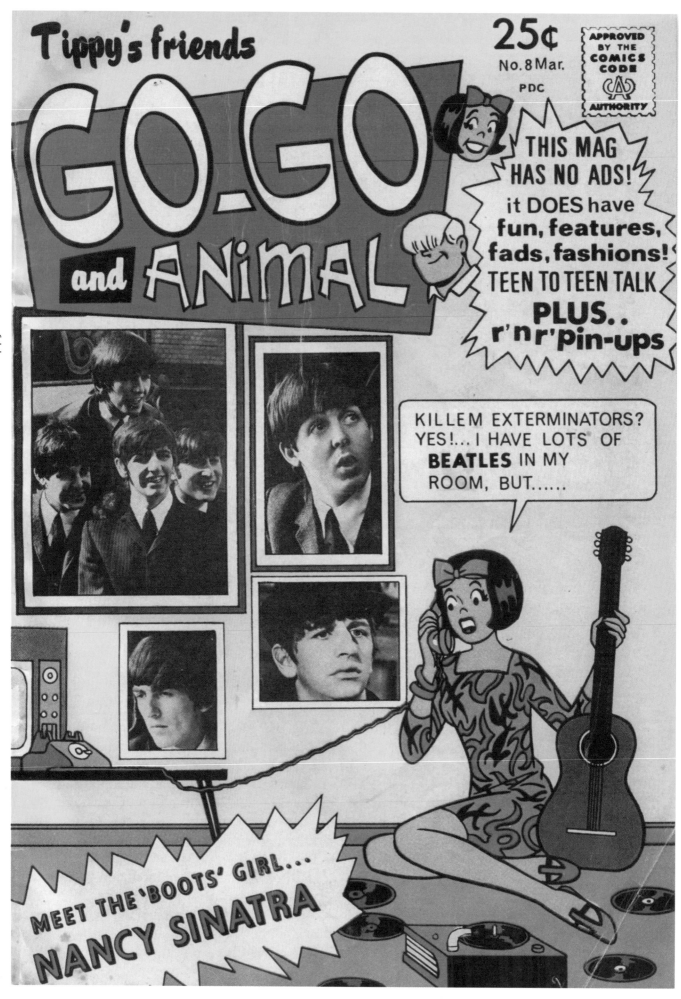

The recent motion picture "WILD IN THE STREETS" came up with a startling observation. Namely, that it's conceivable this country could fall into the hands of adolescents. This is because if America lowered the voting age to 18, there would be more young people voting than old people, and so theoretically, they could vote them-

IF TEENS TOOK OVER

NEW LEADERS WOULD BE ELECTED BY A POPULAR VOTE

JOHN LENNON
as
President

MICHAEL J. POLLARD
as
Vice-President

JOAN BAEZ
as
Secretary of State

TINY TIM
as
Speaker of the House

NEW GOVERNMENT AGENCIES WOULD HAVE TO BE CREATED

C.I.A.
Chicks Intelligence Agency
which will tell all the cats
where the chicks are at.

F____
Far-out B____
which will ____
where the ____

the
____ads
____here
____re.

28

A LOS GRITOS DEL EMPLEADO ACUDIÓ LA POLICÍA Y...

¡QUEDA USTED DESPEDIDO! ¡VAYA VIGILANTE!

PASÓ EL TIEMPO. EN 1925, UN INCENDIO CAUSÓ GRANDES DAÑOS AL MUSEO.

SE LLEVABAN UN BUEN BOTÍN.

YO NO LOS ENVIARÍA A LA CÁRCEL. CON EL SUSTO QUE HAN PASADO YA TIENEN SU MERECIDO.

EN 1928 SE RECONSTRUYÓ EL EDIFICIO Y MADAME TUSSAUD ABRIÓ NUEVAMENTE SUS PUERTAS AL PÚBLICO.

HASTA LA FECHA, LOS TATARANIETOS DE MADAME TUSSAUD HACEN LAS FIGURAS.

"EL VAMPIRO DE LONDRES" PIDIÓ SER MODELADO ANTES DE MORIR (*).

(*). -VÉASE EL No. 148 DE ESTA SERIE.

Y LA SALA DE LAS CELEBRIDADES SE MANTIENE SIEMPRE AL DÍA.

¿UN CIGARRO, RINGO?

SÍ, ESTOS SON DEL TONO DE MIS OJOS.

32

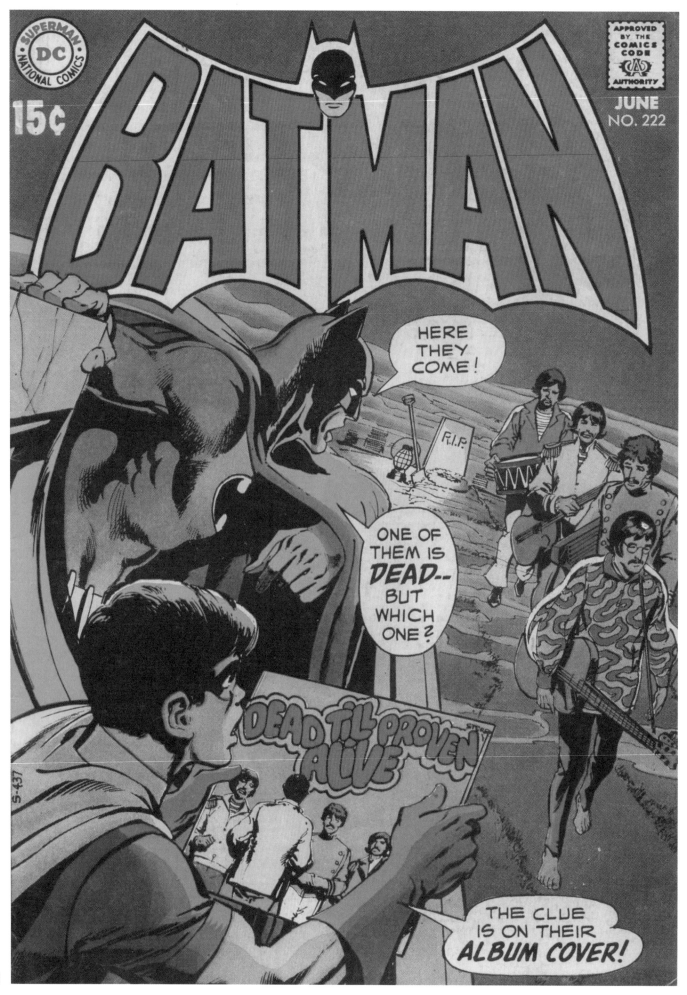

1971–1980

With the end of the sixties and the hippie era, ideologies and hopes foundered "on the hard rocks of reality" and the atmosphere changed. The feeling was that you either had to blow up the system or turn your back on it. It was the decade of Francis Ford Coppola's *Apocalypse Now* and John Landis's *Animal House*, of the Watergate scandal, Bloody Sunday in Northern Ireland, the coup in Chile, and Margaret Thatcher, but also of the discovery, at Afar in Ethiopia on 30 November 1974, of Lucy, the skeleton of an adult female hominid of the apparent age of

WE ALL WANT TO CHANGE THE WORLD

twenty-five who lived at least 3.2 million years ago. The name given to the fossil Australopithecus came from the famous song by The Beatles, which the group of palaeontologists often listened to during breaks in the excavations. In 1978, *Sgt. Pepper's Lonely Hearts Club Band*, the album on which "Lucy in the Sky with Diamonds" was a track, became a film tribute to the Fab Four with music performed by the Bee Gees, Peter Frampton, Aerosmith, Earth Wind & Fire and Toto. A comic strip based on the film would also be published.

the Beatles 1971–1980

1971

30 January. With "My Sweet Lord" George is at number one on the British best-selling singles charts.

15 April. *Let It Be* wins an Oscar in the Original Song Score category.

5 June. *Ram*, credited to Paul and Linda McCartney, reaches number one on the album charts in Great Britain.

1 August. The "Concert for Bangladesh" is staged at Madison Square Garden in New York, a grand benefit event in which Ravi Shankar, Bob Dylan, Eric Clapton, Ringo Starr, Billy Preston and Leon Russell take part. It will be followed shortly afterwards by the release of a triple album.

3 August. Paul announces the formation of his new band, Wings, while arguments and declarations about the end of the story fill the pages of the newspapers. Among the accusations, the harshest comes from John, who claims that McCartney wanted to break the group up back at the time of Epstein's death: "This is just the final act of disintegration."

1972

8 February. The Beatles Fan Club shop closes. At the end of March the offices and secretarial staff also cease their activities.

23 March. Première in New York of the documentary film *The Concert for Bangladesh*.

21 May. The programme *The Beatles Story* is broadcast on BBC's Radio 1.

9 July. Live debut of Wings, at Châteauvallon in France.

1973

2 April. The double compilation albums *The Beatles / 1962–1966* and *The Beatles / 1967–1970* are released simultaneously and enjoy great success internationally: the latter is the group's 15th album to reach number one in the United States.

1974

25 May. George announces the foundation of his record label, Dark Horse: the first artist to sign up is Ravi Shankar.

8–13 July. Paul tops the charts with the album *Band on the Run* both in the US (where he flies to Nashville to produce Peggy Lee's *Let's Love*) and the UK.

26–28 July. The Strawberry Fields Forever Fan Club organizes the first Beatles Convention in Boston.

1975

17 July. Ringo Starr and his wife Maureen get divorced.

19 July. Paul and Wings head the US charts with both the single "Listen to What the Man Said" and the album *Venus and Mars*.

9 September. Wings begins its world tour, lasting thirteen months, in Southampton.

1976

25 January. Ringo is Bob Dylan's guest, in Houston, for the concert organized to show solidarity with the boxer Ruben "Hurricane" Carter. In November he will take part along with many other stars in the farewell concert of The Band at the Winterland Ballroom in San Francisco, filmed by Martin Scorsese (*The Last Waltz*).

3 May. Paul performs live again on an American stage: the "Wings over America" tour starts out from Fort Worth, in Texas.

2 June. Paul's band establishes a record for a paying audience for an indoor concert in Seattle: 67,100.

7 September. George Harrison is found guilty of plagiary: his song "My Sweet Lord" had been copied from a hit by the group The Chiffons, "He's So Fine."

20 September. The promoter of the New York concerts in the years 1964–66, Sid Bernstein, takes out a full-page advertisement in a newspaper asking The Beatles to reunite for a benefit concert. Months earlier they had been offered 30 million dollars for a show: turned down.

25 September. Paul and Wings play in St Mark's Square in Venice for UNESCO.

1977

26 May. The musical *Beatlemania* opens at the Winter Garden Theatre in New York.

4 June. Among the discs that try to win the favour of the "orphaned" fans the most successful is *The Beatles at the Hollywood Bowl*, recorded at the shows staged in 1964–65. Another curiosity is *The Beatles Live! At the Star-Club in Hamburg, Germany 1962*, a compilation of recordings from the early days in Germany.

9 June. George and Patti get divorced.

3 December. "Mull of Kintyre," top of the British charts, becomes the best-selling single of all time, until overtaken by Band Aid's "Do They Know It's Christmas?" in 1984.

1978

1 August. George Harrison's son Dhani is born, and a month later he marries the child's mother Olivia.

30 September. *Sgt. Pepper's Lonely Hearts Club Band*, a film reinterpreting the masterpiece of ten years earlier, is released to cinemas. Produced by Robert Stigwood, it stars the Bee Gees, Peter Frampton and others.

1 December. A boxed set of The Beatles' twelve "British" LPs appears in the shops.

1979

19 May. Big party for the marriage of Eric Clapton and Patti, Harrison's former wife, who tied the knot in Tucson in March: Paul, Ringo and George play together. An almost complete reunion of The Beatles: Jagger, Bowie and Elton John are among the guests.

22 August. Harrison's autobiography, *I Me Mine*, is published in a limited edition of just two thousand copies.

21 September. The secretary general of the United Nations Kurt Waldheim asks the group to stage a benefit concert for the Vietnamese boat people.

24 October. Paul is awarded a special rhodium-plated disc by the Guinness Book of Records as the most successful composer of all time: between 1962 and 1978 he wrote forty-three songs that sold over a million copies each. In addition he has sold over 100 million singles and 100 million albums.

1980

16 January. Paul McCartney is arrested in Japan and held in jail for ten days: he is charged with possession of 219 grams of marijuana.

18 February. Shooting of the film *Caveman* starts in Durango: Ringo Starr will meet his future wife Barbara Bach on the set. Three months later, on 18 May, they will be involved in a serious road accident outside London.

May-September. A series of records are released in memory of The Beatles: *Rarities* and *Beatles Ballads* achieve good sales.

31 October. After a gap of eight years Paul records with George Martin again: they work on "We All Stand Together" in London.

8 December. The murder of John Lennon by a twenty-five-year-old fan, Mark Chapman, who shoots him at the entrance to his residence in New York, the Dakota Building, causes a huge sensation all over the world.

WE LOVE YOU BEATLES

Written and Illustrated by MARGARET SUTTON

JAY KINNEY SPEAKS

ALLATIME, PEOPLE ARE ALWAYS SAYING, "ROCK IS DEAD," "IT'LL NEVER LAST," "BOY, IS ROCK LOUSY LATELY!" AND THE LIKE. I, PERSONALLY REFUSE TO BELIEVE A WORD OF IT. I MEAN, THEY ALWAYS USED TO SAY THE SAME THINGS ABOUT JAZZ . . . AND JUST LOOK AT JAZZ NOW! . . . HMMMM. THEY MAY HAVE A POINT THERE AFTER ALL . . . ANYHOW, HERE'S THE DROOL.

Rock 'n' Roll Forecast 1984

Superstars come and superstars go. Where's Brenda Lee NOW? Chubby Checker? Kookie? Who knows? Furthermore, who cares? But some rock stars do manage to stay in the public eye long past their initial popularity, and 1984 won't be any exception. Frinstance!

John Lennon will have replaced Johnny Carson as night-time TV king.

Mick Jagger and The Rolling Stones will be everyone's favorite Times Square New Year's Eve hosts . . .

However, other present rock stars will have forsaken show business for other life styles altogether . . .

Bob Dylan will have moved to Israel and become a rabbi . . .

Neil Young will be a successful cattle rancher in Argentina.

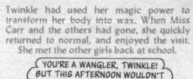

Twinkle had used her magic power to transform her body into wax. When Miss Carr and the others had gone, she quickly returned to normal, and enjoyed the visit. She met the other girls back at school.

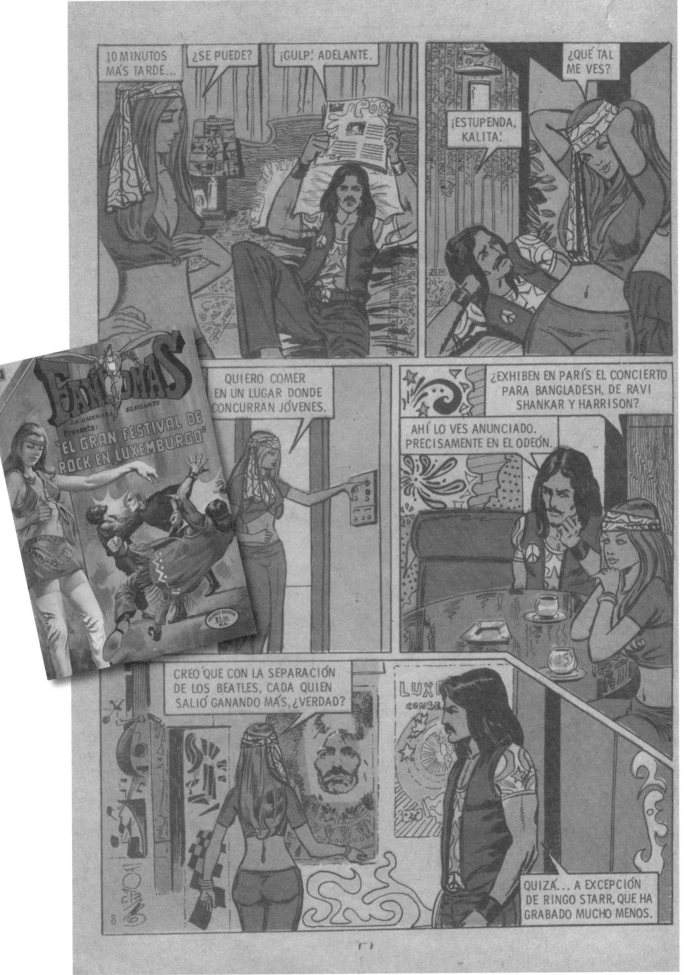

National Lampoon • no. 7 • National Lampoon Inc • USA • 1974

EN ÉCOUTANT DES IMAGES ~IMAGERIE MUSICALE~
SOLÉ & LESUEUR

"RÉTROscisons" UN PEU NOUS AUSSI : PETIT REGARD SUR L'"ÂGE D'OR"... C'EST ARRIVÉ VOUS LE SAVEZ, AU PRINTEMPS 1967 : LE SERGENT PEPPER ET SA FANFARE DU CLUB DES COEURS SOLITAIRES ONT DÉBARQUÉ DANS NOS CONTRÉES. ON L'A DIT ET REDIT, St PEPPER'S LONELY HEARTS CLUB BAND EST UNE SORTE DE CHEF D'OEUVRE. LES BEATLES (car, bien sûr, c' est d'eux, encore, qu'il s'agit) N'EN SONT PAS À UN CHEF D'OEUVRE PRÈS, MAIS CE DISQUE MERVEILLEUX FUT, DANS LE CONTEXTE DE L'ÉPOQUE, L' ÉVÉNEMENT APRÈS LEQUEL TOUT FUT DÉSORMAIS DIFFÉRENT.... LES BEATLES, UNE FOIS DE PLUS, FRAPPÈRENT AU BON MOMENT, CONCRÉTISANT, PAR DES CHANSONS MAGNIFIQUES TOUT LE CLIMAT, L'ATMOSPHÈRE D' UNE PÉRIODE QUI VOYAIT NAÎTRE HENDRIX, LE PSYCHÉDÉLISME, LE MOU- -VEMENT HIPPIE, LES MOUSTACHES, LES COULEURS, LES FESTIVALS, LA FUMÉE...: DÉJÀ AMORCÉ AVEC "REVOLVER", LES BEATLES FIRENT FAIRE À LA MUSIQUE "POP" LE GRAND BOND QUI ALLAIT LUI PERMETTRE DE S'ÉCLA- -TER, DE S'ÉPANOUIR ET DE DEVENIR UNE MUSIQUE RICHE DE MILLE TENDANCES ET APPORTS DIVERS. St PEPPER, SYMBOLISE CETTE RÉVOLUTION MUSICALE (ET SOCIALE) DES ANNÉES 60. POUR ILLUSTRER CETTE PÉRIODE, PRENONS DANS CE DISQUE, UNE CHAN- -SON, COMME ÇA.... DÉLAISSONS POUR CETTE FOIS LES AUTRES "DAMES MUSICALES" DES BEATLES TELLE LA SOLITAIRE ELÉANOR RIGBY, OU MICHELLE (ma belle) OU L'ADORABLE RITA (lovely) OU BIEN ENCORE LA COURAGEUSE LADY MADONNA, AINSI QUE CETTE SACRÉE SEXY DE SADIE, SANS OUBLIER LA CHÈRE PRUDENCE ET MAMAN JULIA... ET AVEC LES GÉNIAUX PAUL, JOHN, GEORGE ET RINGO DRESSONS NOS YEUX ET NOS OREILLES VERS LA PLANANTE ET TRÈS "LENNONIÈNNE":

I'M THE GREATEST !

reconnaissables à leurs moustaches voici le fameux St Pepper et ses amis Paul, John, Ringo (Billy Shears) et George.

LUCY DANS LE CIEL AVEC DES DIAMANTS
lennon/mccartney images SOLÉ 74

DANS UNE BARQUE SUR LA RIVIÈRE, AVEC DES MANDARINIERS ET DES CIELS DE MARMELADE...

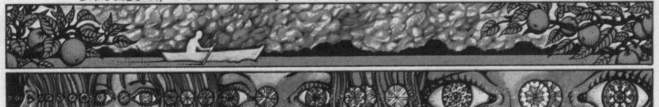

QUELQU'UN VOUS APPELLE, VOUS RÉPONDEZ TRÈS LENTEMENT......... UNE FILLE AUX YEUX DE KALÉIDOSCOPE

Lucy in the Sky with Diamonds

VOUS LA SUIVEZ JUSQU'À UN PONT, PRÈS D'UNE FONTAINE, OÙ DES GENS SUR DES CHEVAUX À BASCULE AVALENT DES TARTES DE GUIMAUVE,

DES FLEURS DE CELLOPHANE VERTES ET JAUNES, PLANENT AU- DESSUS DE VOTRE TÊTE, LE TEMPS D'APERCEVOIR LA FILLE AU SOLEIL DANS LES YEUX, ELLE A DISPARU...

CHACUN VOUS SOURIT QUAND VOUS DÉRIVEZ DEVANT LES FLEURS QUI S'ÉLÈVENT À UNE HAUTEUR VERTIGINEUSE.

①

34

1975 • Pilote • no. 8 new series • Dargaud S.A. Editeur • France

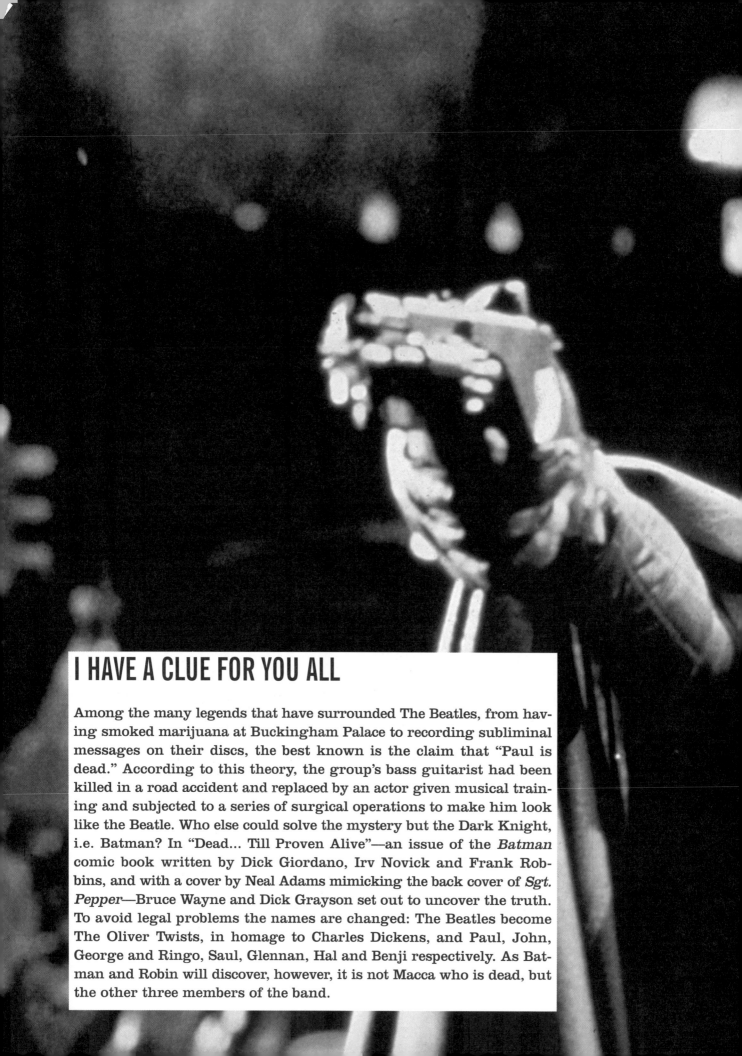

I HAVE A CLUE FOR YOU ALL

Among the many legends that have surrounded The Beatles, from having smoked marijuana at Buckingham Palace to recording subliminal messages on their discs, the best known is the claim that "Paul is dead." According to this theory, the group's bass guitarist had been killed in a road accident and replaced by an actor given musical training and subjected to a series of surgical operations to make him look like the Beatle. Who else could solve the mystery but the Dark Knight, i.e. Batman? In "Dead... Till Proven Alive"—an issue of the *Batman* comic book written by Dick Giordano, Irv Novick and Frank Robbins, and with a cover by Neal Adams mimicking the back cover of *Sgt. Pepper*—Bruce Wayne and Dick Grayson set out to uncover the truth. To avoid legal problems the names are changed: The Beatles become The Oliver Twists, in homage to Charles Dickens, and Paul, John, George and Ringo, Saul, Glennan, Hal and Benji respectively. As Batman and Robin will discover, however, it is not Macca who is dead, but the other three members of the band.

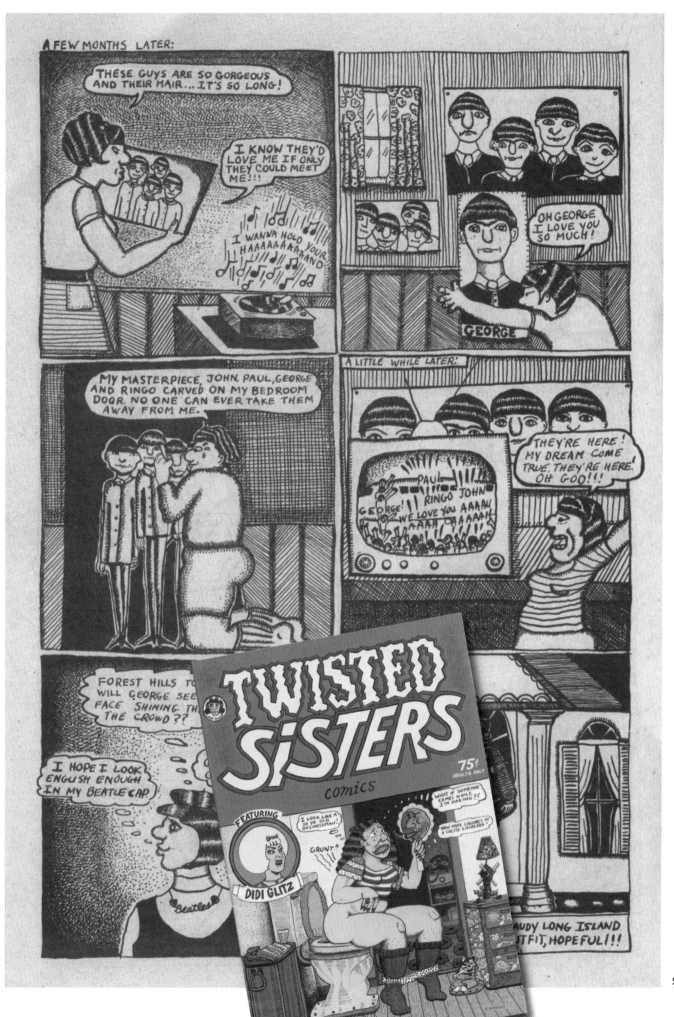

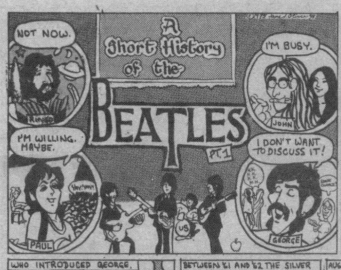

National Lampoon • special October issue • National Lampoon Inc • USA • **1977**

LEAVING THEIR CREATOR TO NURSE HIS WOUNDS AND MOURN HIS LOSS, THE BEATLES ESCAPED DOWN HAMBURG'S REEPERBAHN.

FREE FROM THE EVIL CLUTCHES OF DR. EPSTEIN, THEY RETURNED TO LIVERPOOL AND MODEST SUCCESS.

PLEASE PLEASE ME, OH YEAH LIKE I PLEASE YOU..!

DR. EPSTEIN RECOVERED FROM HIS INJURIES, AND THOUGH HIS MOP-TOPS HAD TURNED AGAINST HIM, HE SOUGHT MANY TIMES TO WIN THEM BACK.

I WILL ALWAYS LOVE YOU BOYS. LOOK, I'VE GOTTEN YOU A RECORDING CONTRACT AND THREE APPEARANCES ON THE ED SULLIVAN SHOW!

WE'LL TAKE THE CONTRACT AND THE ED SULLIVAN GIG, EPSTEIN.

BUT YOU'RE STILL A BLOODY BUM FUCKER!

I SIMPLY MUST HAVE THAT SHORT ONE!

CHARMINGLY PLEASANT IN A DREADFUL WAY!

I'VE SIGNED YOU TO DO A FILM - LET'S GO TO SPAIN AND CELEBRATE.

GO FUCK YER MUM!

BLOODY LIMP WRIST.

HYDROCEPHALIC SNOT BAG.

YEAH, YEAH, YEAH!

BUT FOR ALL OF HIS EFFORTS, DR. EPSTEIN WOULD FAIL, FOR HE HAD TAMPERED WITH LIFE, AND MORE IMPORTANTLY... ROCK 'N' ROLL.

BRIAN'S GETTIN' TO BE A BLOODY DRAG.

HE'S GOT US RICH AND FAMOUS, ALRIGHT, BUT STILL...

MAYBE WE OUGHTA...

WHAT?

THE END

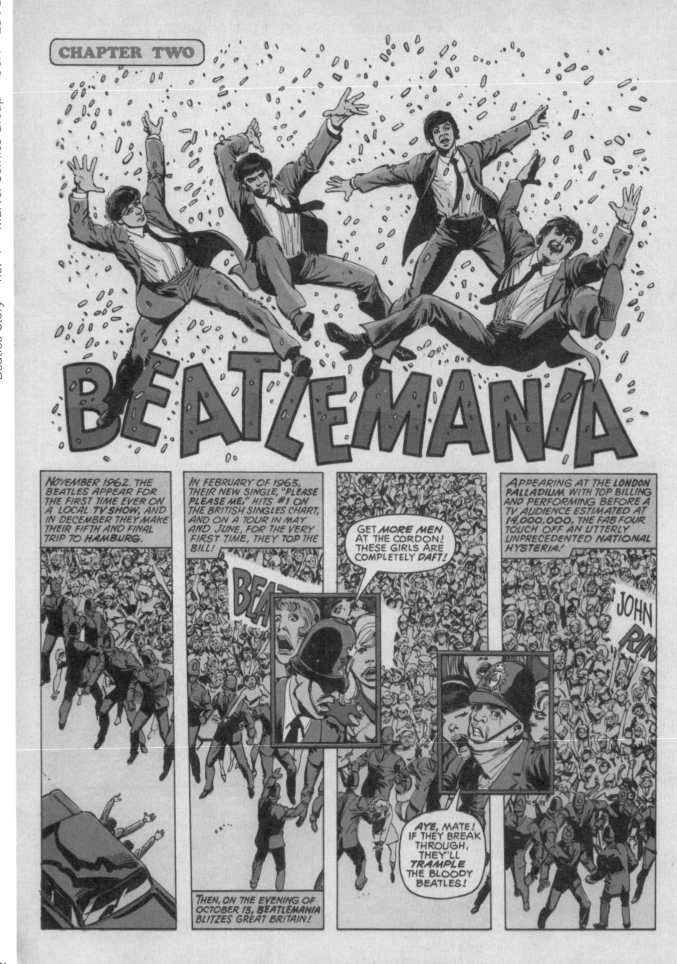

MAIS JOHN N'EST PAS LE SEUL À FAIRE DES HISTOIRES...

HÉ, LES ENFANTS, REGARDEZ CETTE NOTE DE SERVICE ET PLEUREZ.

GEORGE HARRISON À TOUT LE PERSONNEL DE APPLE: DOUZE ANGES DE L'ENFER ARRIVERONT À APPLE LA SEMAINE PROCHAINE.

ESSAYEZ DE LES AIDER AU MAXIMUM SANS POUR AUTANT NÉGLIGER VOTRE SERVICE.

LES AIDER À FAIRE QUOI ?

ET, À LA MI-DÉCEMBRE, ILS ARRIVENT.

NOUS SOMMES...HUM... TRÈS HONORÉS DE VOUS RECEVOIR...

ENFIN... JE CROIS.

NE VOUS VEXEZ PAS, MAIS GEORGE N'EST PAS LÀ AUJOURD'HUI.

LES COPAINS DE FRISCO NOUS ONT DIT QUE C'ÉTAIT UN MEC SYMPA.

AU FAIT... EST-CE QUE VOUS N'ÉTIEZ PAS CENSÉS ÊTRE... DOUZE ?

OUAIS, C'EST ÇA, MAIS ON VIENT D'ABORD À DEUX POUR VOIR COMMENT EST LE COIN.

EN DÉPIT DE LEURS MANIÈRES TERRIFIANTES ET DE LEUR AFFREUSE RÉPUTATION, LES ANGES DE L'ENFER NE DÉVASTENT PAS LES BUREAUX DE APPLE.

ILS RESTENT JUSTE ASSEZ POUR ASSISTER À LA GRANDE FÊTE DE NOËL DE BIG APPLE AVANT DE RENTRER AUX U.S.A.

JOHN ET YOKO APPARAISSENT À CETTE RÉCEPTION, CETTE FOIS EN VÊTEMENTS DE GALA.

JOYEUX NOËL, JOYEUSES PÂQUES, JOYEUX N'IMPORTE QUOI À VOUS TOUS !

ET POURTANT, DERRIÈRE CETTE ATMOSPHÈRE DE FÊTE TRÈS GAIE, LA TENSION DEMEURE CONSTANTE.

CHAQUE ANNÉE, DEPUIS 1963, LES BEATLES ONT SORTI UN DISQUE SPÉCIAL DE NOËL POUR LES MEMBRES DE LEURS CLUBS DE FANS. CETTE ANNÉE NE FERA PAS EXCEPTION.

COMMENT ÇA VA LES GARS ?

LES DÉLAIS ÉTAIENT SERRÉS, PAUL, MAIS LES EXPÉDITIONS [...] PARTIES [...]

EN JANVIER 1969, LES BEATLES SONT À NOUVEAU RÉUNIS. L'IDÉE EST DE REVENIR À LA BASE ET DE RETROUVER LEURS RACINES PROFONDES

NOUS SOMMES DEVENUS BEAUCOUP TROP UN ORCHESTRE DE STUDIO... SURIMPRESSIONS PAR-CI, PISTES MULTIPLES PAR LÀ...

CE QUI MANQUE C'EST LE VIEUX STYLE BEATLE.

ON EST D'ACCORD, PAUL.

[...] VONT ENREGISTRER UN DISQUE DE [...] MAIS ILS FERONT FILMER TOUTE LA [...] DOCUMENTAIRE.

[...]EST LE SEUL À GARDER SON [...]JET PROGRESSE PÉNIBLEMENT [...]MIS EN SOMMEIL.

PENDANT CE TEMPS, LA COMPTABILITÉ RÉVÈLE QUE DES SOMMES STUPÉFIANTES DISPARAISSENT À APPLE.

[...]NE SUFFISAIT PAS, [...]E DES BEATLES POUR [...] CONTRÔLE FINANCIER [...]AGNIE D'ÉDITIONS MUSI[...]URTE À L'OPPOSITION DE [...]MÉCHANTS BLEUS.

C'EST LE COMMENCEMENT D'UNE SÉRIE DE COMPLICATIONS LÉGALES TRÈS EMBROUILLÉES. C'EST AUSSI LE COMMENCEMENT DE LA FIN.

With the huge success of "Beatlemania" and the hulabaloo about the movie, "Sgt. Pepper's Lonely Hearts Club Band," fans seem to be demanding that "The Beatles" themselves return and make the scene again. Yet, with the constantly changing trends in the industry, we wonder how they might make out. . .

If The Beatles Decided To Try A Comeback

BOULDER MUSIC CO. home of HARD ROCK NED NEANDERTHAL president

Come on in, guys. You're just in time to listen to my latest invention—an L.P. record that plays twice as fast as a 33 ⅓ — so that you can't tell what classical composer it was stolen from. I'll tune this out in a minute and tune you into what's happening with the newest in music—the "New Wave."

You mean "Punk Rock?"

Exactly. And I've come up with the biggest punks of all time. As you know, many Punkers wear German World War II outfits. Well, Ned Neanderthal has done it again. My latest discovery is an original German World War II outfit—"Martin Bormann And The Panzer Division!"

LOUD   LOUDER   LOUDEST

POP   KRAKLE   SCRATCH

You've got to be kidding!

FREE! ELEPHANT-SIZE POSTER

TRASH

ALL THE JUNK UNFIT TO PRINT

. . .And yucch it u
MONS

We have low-anxiety fun with
THE BEATLES,
CALIFORNIA,
A GODFATHER

INSIDE
NORMAN
NEBISH'S
HEAD
A WEIRD
JOURNEY INTO
INNER SPACE

RECORDING ROYALTIES

47

THE PICTS, UNDER THE CONTROL OF THE DRUIDS WERE THE TOUGHEST FIGHTING FORCE THE ROMAN SOLDIERS EVER FACED. ONE PICT WOULD DELIBERATELY JUMP ON A ROMAN SPEAR TO LET THE PICT BEHIND HIM KILL THE ROMAN SOLDIER.

IT WAS AROUND *98 - 180 A.D. THAT THE DRUID RELIGION WAS OUTLAWED. IT WENT UNDERGROUND AND HAS BEEN SECRETLY ACTIVE ALL THIS TIME.

*"DECLINE AND FALL OF THE ROMAN EMPIRE," BY EDWARD GIBBON, VOL. I, CHAPTER 2, PAGE 32.

LANCE, WHAT KIND OF MUSICAL INSTRUMENTS DID THE DRUIDS HAVE?

THEY USED A FLUTE, A TAMBOURINE AND A DRUM COVERED WITH HUMAN HIDE!

THE WORDS TO EVERY SONG OR MELODY WERE FOR CASTING SPELLS... THE DRUM BEAT WAS THE KEY TO ADDICT THE LISTENER...A FORM OF HYPNOTISM...THE SAME BEAT THE DRUIDS USED IS IN THE ROCK MUSIC OF TODAY...BOTH HARD AND SOFT ROCK, THE BEAT IS *STILL* THERE!

LET ME TELL YOU, GENTLEMEN, THE BEATLES OPENED UP A PANDORA'S BOX WHEN THEY HIT THE UNITED STATES WITH THEIR DRUID/ROCK BEAT IN THE 1960'S.

THEN THEY BECAME SO POPULAR THAT THEY WERE ABLE TO TURN OUR YOUNG PEOPLE ON TO THE EASTERN RELIGIONS. THE FLOOD GATES TO WITCHCRAFT WERE OPENED. THE U.S. WILL NEVER RECOVER . . . IT WAS WELL PLANNED.

ONE OF THE GREATEST VICTORIES IN THE OCCULT WORLD WAS TO PENETRATE THE "CHRISTIAN" MUSIC WITH THEIR SATANIC BEAT.

I KNOW OF CHRISTIAN KIDS WHO DESTROYED THEIR ROCK RECORDS, BUT AFTER LISTENING TO "CHRISTIAN" ROCK, THE DRUID BEAT SOON PULLED THEM BACK TO WORLDLY ROCK MUSIC AGAIN...

THEN THE DESIRE TO STUDY THE BIBLE COOLS OFF!

16

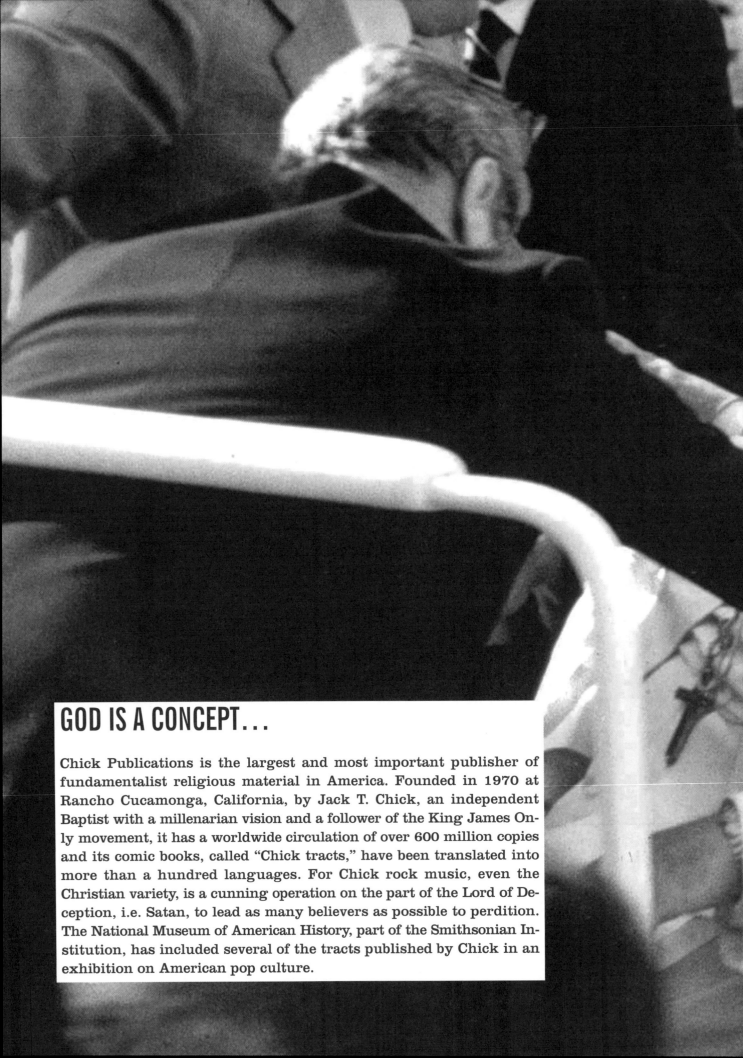

GOD IS A CONCEPT...

Chick Publications is the largest and most important publisher of fundamentalist religious material in America. Founded in 1970 at Rancho Cucamonga, California, by Jack T. Chick, an independent Baptist with a millenarian vision and a follower of the King James Only movement, it has a worldwide circulation of over 600 million copies and its comic books, called "Chick tracts," have been translated into more than a hundred languages. For Chick rock music, even the Christian variety, is a cunning operation on the part of the Lord of Deception, i.e. Satan, to lead as many believers as possible to perdition. The National Museum of American History, part of the Smithsonian Institution, has included several of the tracts published by Chick in an exhibition on American pop culture.

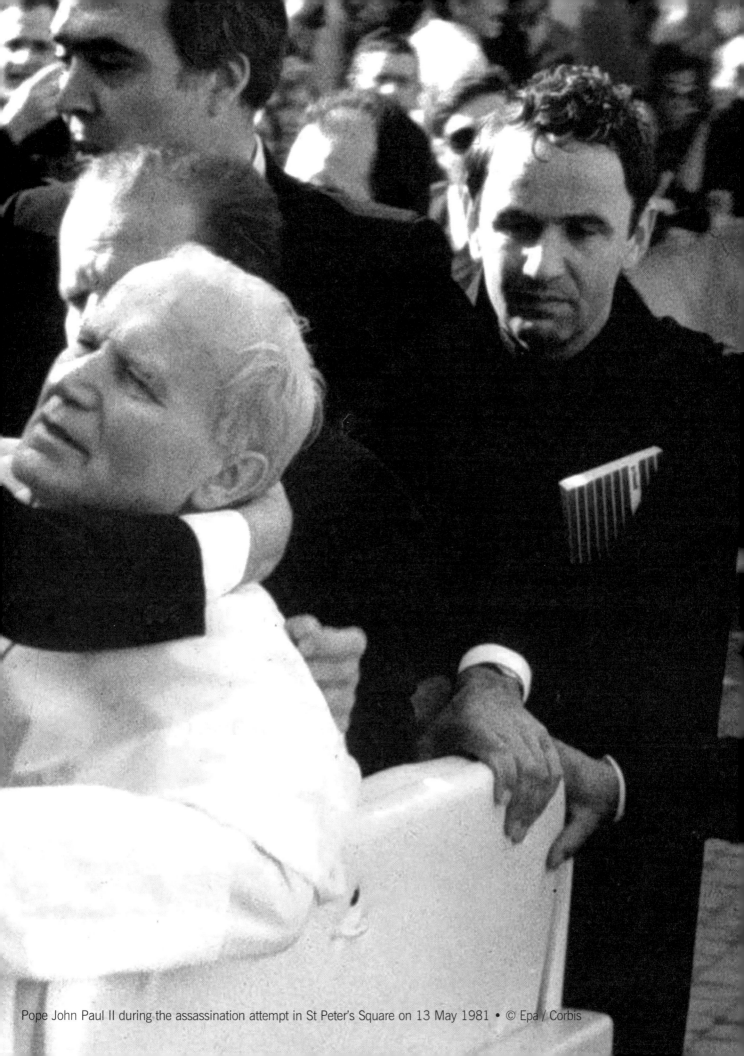

Pope John Paul II during the assassination attempt in St Peter's Square on 13 May 1981 • © Epa / Corbis

14

1979 • Fluide Glacial • no. 36 • Edition Audi S.A.S. • France

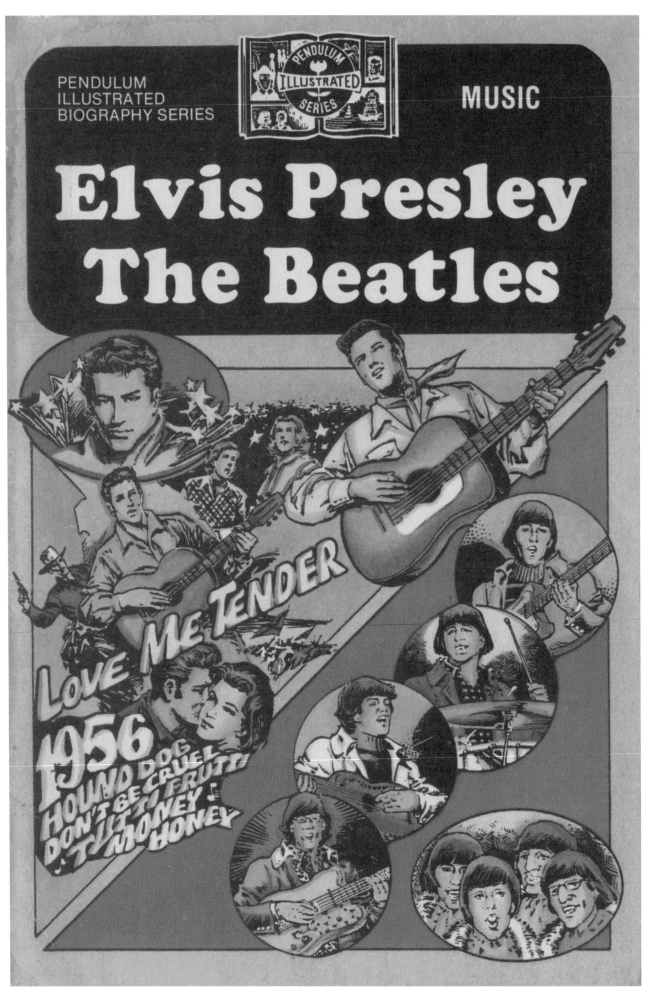

Out at Paul's ranch, the boys dug out all their old uniforms and equipment. For six hours they played every song they ever wrote. It was a Beatle fan's dream come true - but somehow their hearts weren't really in it....

To make a long story one frame shorter, the Fab-Four thought it was a great idea. They never did like the reunion stipulation that they play exactly like they did in the 60's. Sue began a crash course. Every night they hung out in the honkytonks...

13

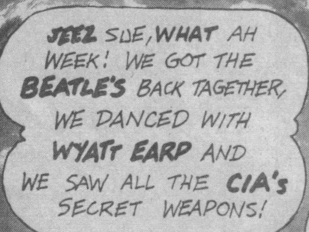

Il Male n. 48 Anno III 22 dicembre 1980 Sped. in abb. post. gr. II/70 L. 700

1980 • Il Male • Italy

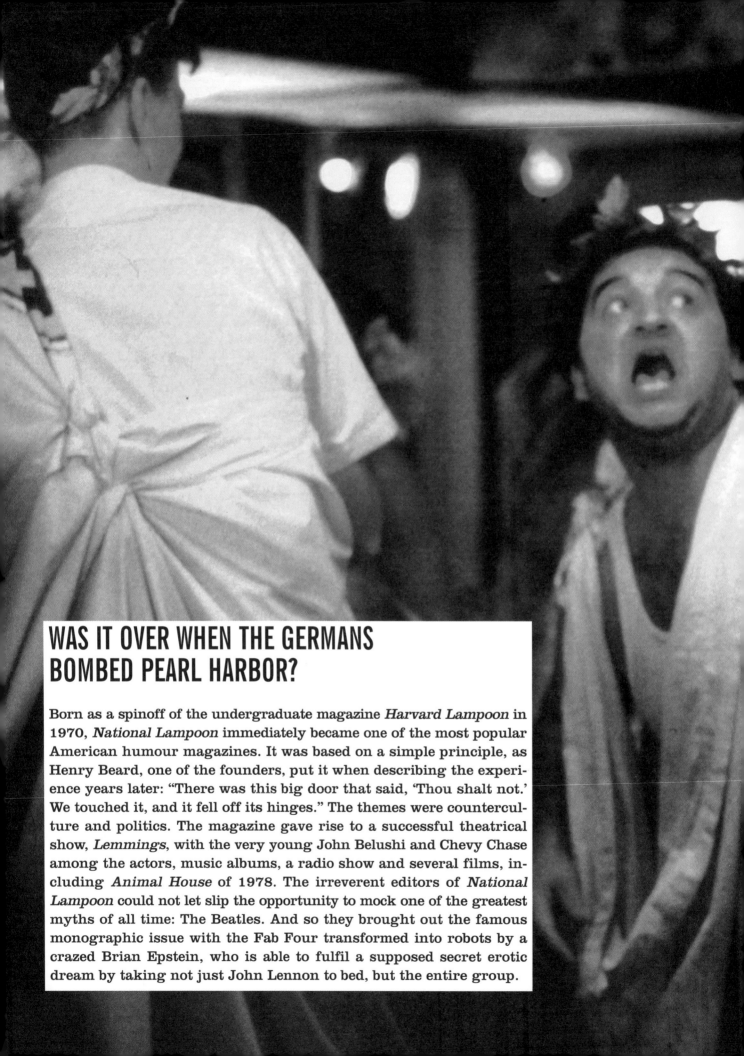

WAS IT OVER WHEN THE GERMANS BOMBED PEARL HARBOR?

Born as a spinoff of the undergraduate magazine *Harvard Lampoon* in 1970, *National Lampoon* immediately became one of the most popular American humour magazines. It was based on a simple principle, as Henry Beard, one of the founders, put it when describing the experience years later: "There was this big door that said, 'Thou shalt not.' We touched it, and it fell off its hinges." The themes were counterculture and politics. The magazine gave rise to a successful theatrical show, *Lemmings*, with the very young John Belushi and Chevy Chase among the actors, music albums, a radio show and several films, including *Animal House* of 1978. The irreverent editors of *National Lampoon* could not let slip the opportunity to mock one of the greatest myths of all time: The Beatles. And so they brought out the famous monographic issue with the Fab Four transformed into robots by a crazed Brian Epstein, who is able to fulfil a supposed secret erotic dream by taking not just John Lennon to bed, but the entire group.

John Belushi in a scene from the film *Animal House* • 1978 • © UNIVERSAL PICTURES - Album / CONTRASTO

1981—1990

After years of legal battles Jon Wiener, a university professor of history and author of the book *Gimme Some Truth: The John Lennon FBI Files*, succeeded in getting the secret dossier on the musician declassified. What has been called the "Watergate of rock & roll" began when President Richard "Tricky Dick" Nixon and Edgar J. Hoover, director of the Federal Bureau of Investigation, decided that the former Beatle, who had just moved to America, was a "dangerous extremist" who needed watching. In 1972 the news came out of "a donation of 75,000 dollars by Lennon to an organization that intended to disrupt the Republican Convention" of that year and the pressure was stepped up. The surveillance continued un-

LIKE THE FBI
AND THE CIA...

til 1975, when John Lennon and Yoko Ono obtained green cards, but were not allowed to see the documents that concerned them. In the end only Wiener's tenacity was able to make a breach in the wall; no simple matter, as the professor recalls: "Early in 1981, shortly after John Lennon's murder on December 8, 1980, I filed a Freedom of Information Act (FOIA) request for any files the FBI had kept on Lennon." The FBI released only a few of the documents in May. Wiener then filed a lawsuit, asking the federal judge to order the Bureau to release ALL of the documents. This was the start of a 14-year court battle, begun under Reagan as president and ending under Clinton. Better late than never.

the Beatles 1981–1990

1981

27 April. Ringo and Barbara Bach marry in London. Paul comes to the wedding. Relations are repaired between the two of them and George Harrison: they collaborate on Ringo's new album, *Stop and Smell the Roses*.

1982

24 April. At the top of the world hit parade is "Ebony and Ivory," written by Paul and sung as a duet with Stevie Wonder. The album released shortly afterwards, *Tug of War*, proves a similar success. As a mark of his great energy in this period, a few months later he will also record a duet with Michael Jackson, "The Girl Is Mine," on the record-breaking album *Thriller*.

10 September. Recordings of The Beatles' unsuccessful audition at Decca emerge from the archives: they are released on the LP *The Complete Silver Beatles*.

30 October. On the twentieth anniversary of "Love Me Do" all of The Beatles' singles are re-released, and once again sell in large numbers.

1983

19 November. TV launch of Paul and Michael Jackson's video, *Say Say Say*, which has cost the record sum of 500,000 dollars. It is the trailer for McCartney's new album, *Pipes of Peace*, on which many guests play. Paul writes the theme music for the film *The Honorary Consul*, starring Richard Gere.

1984

16 January. More trouble for Paul and Linda, who are arrested and fined in Barbados for possession of drugs.

9 April. The Beatle City exhibition centre opens in Liverpool.

3 November. *Give My Regards to Broad Street* tops the British album charts. It is the soundtrack of the film of the same name starring Paul McCartney: the film will get negative reviews and a lukewarm reception from the public.

1985

18 January. Produced by Harrison's own production company, HandMade Films, *Water* is premièred in London, Harrison himself appears in a scene at the United Nations, along with Ringo Starr and Eric Clapton. George also wrote a song for the soundtrack, "Focus of Attention."

13 July. At the climax of the Live Aid concert at Wembley Stadium, London, Paul sings "Let It Be."

10 August. Michael Jackson buys the copyrights to The Beatles' song catalogue, paying 47.5 million dollars. Paul is very unhappy about the move.

7 September. Ringo is the first of The Beatles to become a grandfather: the child, Zak's daughter, is called Tatya Jane. Ringo and Zak, also a drummer, will contribute to Little Steven's project "Artists United Against Apartheid," trailered by the single "Sun City."

1986

September. After Harrison appears as a guest on Duane Eddy's self-titled album, his HandMade Films' most ambitious production (in which he appears in a cameo role and on the soundtrack) reaches the screens. "Shanghai Surprise" starring Madonna and Sean Penn is panned by the critics.

1987

7 March. Lennon and McCartney are the first non-American authors to be inducted into the Songwriters Hall of Fame, while The Beatles' catalogue starts to come out on CD.

5–6 June. George and Ringo are among the participants in the annual Prince's Trust Rock Gala at Wembley Arena: together they perform "While My Guitar Gently Weeps" and "Here Comes the Sun."

13 June. On the twentieth anniversary of its release, *Sgt. Pepper* is back in the British charts, at number three.

1988

20 January. Ceremony at the Waldorf Astoria in New York for the induction of The Beatles into the Rock and Roll Hall of Fame, in the presence of George, Ringo and Yoko Ono. Paul's absence stirs controversy.

February. The video of 'When We Was Fab', written by George Harrison and Jeff Lynne, is shown on TV: Ringo Starr also appears in it.

8 September. The Hard Rock Cafe chain acquires the bus used for the film *Magical Mystery Tour*.

23 September. A fundamental book for all enthusiasts and collectors comes out: edited by the historian Mark Lewisohn, *The Complete Beatles Recording Sessions* reconstructs the Fab Four's entire recording activity. It supplements a similar volume published in 1986, by the same author and devoted to their concerts, *The Beatles Live!*.

October. An exceptional supergroup hiding behind the name of Traveling Wilburys releases its debut album, *Vol. 1*: the members are Harrison, Lynne, Bob Dylan, Roy Orbison and Tom Petty.

1989

February. Paul releases ("Back in the USSR") on the Russian state label Melodiya, an album in which he plays around with reminiscences of rock & roll, reviving songs like "Lucille," "Ain't That a Shame," "Lawdy, Miss Clawdy," "Kansas City"... There is a rush to get hold of the first copies, intended solely for the Soviet market.

20 April. With fellow musicians from Liverpool, Gerry Marsden, Holly Johnson and The Christians, Paul records a benefit single, "Ferry 'cross the Mersey,"

March. George is a guest on albums by Tom Petty (*Full Moon Fever*) and Eric Clapton (*Journeyman*); he also writes "Cheer Down," on the soundtrack of *Lethal Weapon 2*.

24 June. At number one in the British charts, *Flowers in the Dirt* is a product of the partnership between Paul McCartney and Elvis Costello.

23 July. Live comeback in grand style for Ringo Starr and His All-Starr Band in Dallas, Texas: members of the group include Dr John, Joe Walsh, Rick Danko, Levon Helm, Clarence Clemons, Nils Lofgren...

28 September. Paul's first world tour in thirteen years opens in Gothenburg, Sweden.

1990

February. Paul records "It's Now or Ever," Presley's version of "O sole mio," for *The Last Temptation of Elvis*, a tribute album in the singer's memory.

12 April. Asteroids 4147–50, discovered in 1983 and 1984 by astronomers Brian Skiff and Edward Bowell of the Lowell Observatory in Flagstaff, Arizona, are renamed Lennon, McCartney, Harrison and Starr.

21 April. McCartney enters the Guinness Book of Records for the biggest paying audience of all time, 184,000 people at the Maracanã Stadium in Rio de Janeiro. The previous record had been achieved by Frank Sinatra on 26 January 1980, at the same venue.

5 May. Ringo Starr takes part in the "John Lennon Tribute," along with dozens of other artists: for the occasion he has recorded "I Call Your Name" with Jeff Lynne, Tom Petty, Joe Walsh and Jim Keltner.

September. Following the compilation of charts to list the most played songs in history, "Michelle" and "Something" receive awards for each having been played over 4 million times on radio and TV: "Yesterday" exceeds 5 million.

November. *Traveling Wilburys Vol. 3*, the intentionally misnumbered second album by Harrison, Dylan and co. (minus Roy Orbison who had died in December 1988), is released and sees a fair measure of success.

JOHN LENNON (illustration Liz Bijl)

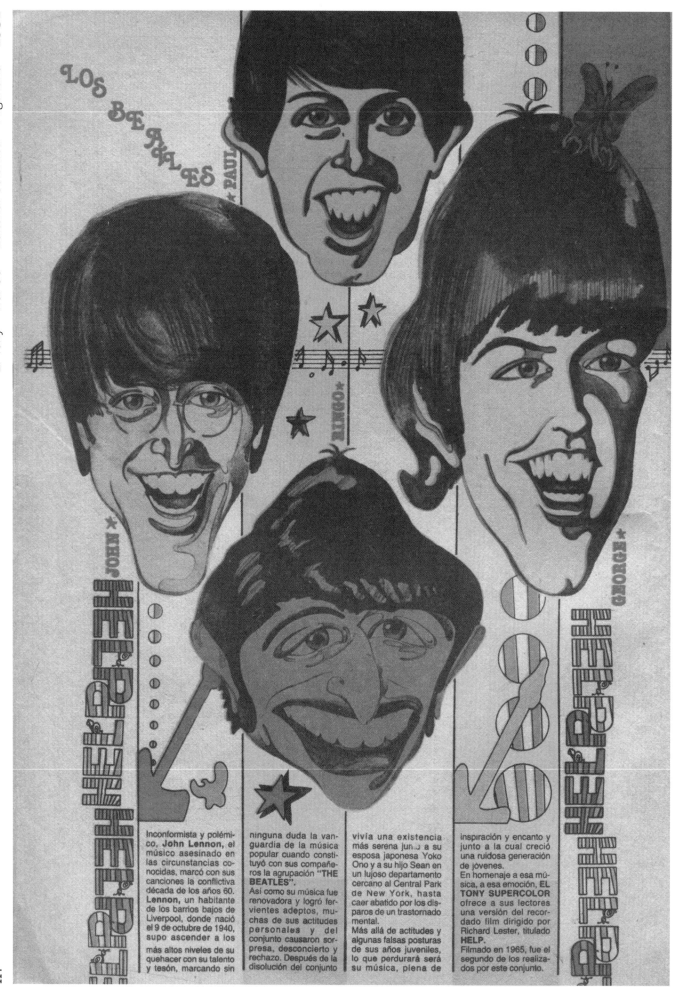

Inconformista y polémico, **John Lennon**, el músico asesinado en las circunstancias conocidas, marcó con sus canciones la conflictiva década de los años 60. **Lennon**, un habitante de los barrios bajos de Liverpool, donde nació el 9 de octubre de 1940, supo ascender a los más altos niveles de su quehacer con su talento y tesón, marcando sin

ninguna duda la vanguardia de la música popular cuando constituyó con sus compañeros la agrupación **"THE BEATLES"**.
Así como su música fue renovadora y logró fervientes adeptos, muchas de sus actitudes personales y del conjunto causaron sorpresa, desconcierto y rechazo. Después de la disolución del conjunto

vivía una existencia más serena junto a su esposa japonesa Yoko Ono y a su hijo Sean en un lujoso departamento cercano al Central Park de New York, hasta caer abatido por los disparos de un trastornado mental.
Más allá de actitudes y algunas falsas posturas de sus años juveniles, lo que perdurará será su música, plena de

inspiración y encanto y junto a la cual creció una ruidosa generación de jóvenes.
En homenaje a esa música, a esa emoción, **EL TONY SUPERCOLOR** ofrece a sus lectores una versión del recordado film dirigido por Richard Lester, titulado **HELP**.
Filmado en 1965, fue el segundo de los realizados por este conjunto.

1981 • Tintin • no. 5 • Dargaud S.A. Editeur • France

37

ISSN 0712-7774

AARDVARK-VANAHEIM PRESENTS

CEREBUS

36
MAR

$1.50

THE NIGHT BEFORE

PERCHE' NON ME L'HAI DETTO SUBITO CHE ERI TU LA RAGAZZA NELLA SOFFITTA CON PAUL McCARTNEY?

DAI, REMO... MI CHIEDI PERCHE'?

...MA RICORDATI CHE PAUL CI TIENE A TE...

...COME AMICO...

CIAO, BARBRA...

L'ESTATE BLOCCO' OGNI MIA ATTIVITA' MUSICALE. OZIAVO IN NEGOZIO, MENTRE RORY E I RAGAZZI SUONAVANO GIU' AL CAMPEGGIO DI BUTLIN...

UN GIORNO PERO' MI CHIAMARONO PER INFORMARMI DI UNA NOVITA' NELLA FORMAZIONE...

ABBIAMO CAMBIATO IL BATTERISTA?... E RINGO?

ERANO VENUTI A TROVARMI. VEDENDOLI ASSIEME D'UN TRATTO PER LA PRIMA VOLTA, INTUII QUALCOSA DI CIO' CHE SAREBBE SUCCESSO...

VISTO CHE BEI VESTITI CI HA FATTO METTERE EPSTEIN?

SENTII CHE I TEMPI SAREBBERO CAMBIATI VELOCEMENTE E MI DISSI: "OK, SONO PRONTO."

RICORDATI! IL DISCO ESCE IL 4 OTTOBRE!!

MERTOUR

TEND.

YEAHYEAHYEAH

87

THE TOPPERMOST OF THE POPPERMOST

An elegant black-and-white and unusual atmospheres, a precise and distinctive line and a style described as photorealistic, combined with an exceptional script, are the elements that characterize *The Beatles. Their Story in Pictures*, the graphic novel written by Angus Allan, author among other things of texts for *Danger Mouse*, *Logan's Run* and *Charlie's Angels*, and drawn by Arthur Ranson, creator of the *Sapphire & Steele*, *Duckula* and *Dr Who* comic strips, to mention just the best-known. The result? Surprising. First published in episodes in the British magazine *Look-in* and then in a small volume, the story would set a trend, becoming a classic. An Italian version in colour would come out in the eighties.

EXCLUSIVE - THE POP SCOOP OF THE CENTURY!!

THE BEATLES ARE BACK!

'Fab Four' re-form
-new album due

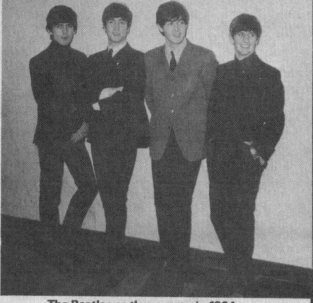

The Beatles as they were - in 1964

Yes, it's true. Fifteen years after they split up pop legends The Beatles are set to reform. And work on a new album is already underway.

Surviving members of the most successful pop group in the history of the world have consistently denied rumours that the band had been planning a comeback. But it now seems certain that the best selling artists ever in the history of popular music will soon be back in business.

LIVERPOOL

The mastermind behind the move is Johnny Johnson, a Liverpool based plumber and life long fan of the fab four. He spoke to us from a recording studio in London where work has already begun on a new Beatles L.P.

"It just seemed right after all this time that the band shou[ld] get together again", he told u[s.] "Obviously there were problem[s] and bearing in mind the sa[d]

'It just seemed right after all this time'

loss of John Lennon there was a need for a new guitarist and songwriter. The obvious choi[ce] was John's son Juli[an...] him[...]

Unfortunately none of the remaining Beatles, Paul McCartney, George Harrison and Ringo Starr were interested and so Johnson had to recruit a further three musicians before rehearsals could begin.

"I decided to do the singing myself so I really only needed another two", he explained.

LIVERPOOL

"I put an ad. in the Liverpool Echo and got fixed up with a drummer straight aw[ay...] he knew a bas[s...] [w]orking [...]arted [...]

"All the material on the album is going to be new stuff, and I can already see a change in musical direction beginning to come through," Johnny told us.

"The old stuff still stands the tests of time, but there's a lot of new ideas coming through and I think a few of our fans might be pleasantly surprised with the results."

STRAWBERRY

If you were too young to catch The Beatles first time round, you'll have a chance to see them on their comback tour which will be timed to coincide with the release of their new album. The L.P., which is due in the shops by mid-1986, is provisionally titled 'Strawberry Roads Tomorrow'.

professo[r...] [...] PARTIAL [...]ess.

OKAY JOE, READY TO TEST MY NEW ACID RESISTANT SOCKS!

Storia del Rock • by Serge Dutfoy, Dominique Farran and Michael Sadler • Mondadori • Italy • **1985**

RINGO AND AUNTIE JESSIE ARE ALWAYS QUARRELING ABOUT ONE THING OR THE OTHER. BUT THEY BOTH AGREE IT WOULD BE EXCITING TO GO ON A MYSTERY TOUR... A *MAGICAL MYSTERY TOUR!!!*

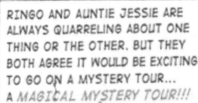

YOU'VE GONE TOO FAR!!!

STRANGELY ENOUGH, THREE OTHER KITTLES DECIDE TO GO ON A MAGICAL MYSTERY TOUR AS WELL, SO THEY ALL CLIMB ABOARD THE *B-I-G* YELLOW AND BLUE BUS AS JOLLY JIMMY JOHNSON (THE COURIER) AND WENDY WINTERS (THE DELIGHTFUL TOUR HOSTESS) INTRODUCE THEMSELVES!

OH MY! LOOKEE FELLAS!

♫ GOOD MORNING! ♫

WELCOME TO MAGICAL MYSTERY TOUR! IS EVERYBODY *COMFY?*

THE FUR FAB FOUR FROM LITTERBOX, ENGLAND! THE KITTLES MAGICAL MYSTERY TOUR

NOT TAKING YOU WITH ME *ANYMORE!*

BOUGHT THE TICKETS? I DID!

YES, YOU BOUGHT THE TICKETS - BUT WITH *MY MONEY!*

CLIMBING ABOARD THE BUS AUNTIE JESSIE AND RINGO CONTINUE TO ARGUE AS JOHN, PAUL AND GEORGE LOOK FOR THEIR SEATS!

HEY RINGO, WHO'S THE *BLIMP?*

HEY AUNTIE! YOU'VE GONE TOO FAR!!!

HURRY LADS! LET'S GET OUR SEATS BEFORE SHE TAKES THE LOT OF THEM!

HAR! HAR! GOOD ONE JOHN!

THEN JOLLY JIMMY (THE COURIER) SMILES CHEERFULLY AS THE BUS BEGINS TO MOVE WITH A STEADY "SWOOOOSH!" AS THE KITTLES NESTLE INTO THEIR APPROPIATE SEATS. TEA AND CHIPS ARE SERVED, AND A MILLION OR SO HUNGRY PEOPLE (IT SEEMS) BEGIN TO CLANK FORKS AND KNIVES READY FOR BREAKFAST!

WATCH IT LADS! I'VE HEARD THESE MAGICAL MYSTERY TOURS CAN BECOME PRETTY STRANGE!

Underground Surrealist Magazine

$2.00

#3 Summer 1988

brings you more cartoons than any Boston publication

THE DAY THE STOCK MARKET CRASHED

RAMESES THE GREAT AND CARTOONS ABOUT ANCIENT EGYPT

THE HARMONIC CONVERGENCE; AN EYEWITNESS REPORT

Tutto Musica & Spettacolo • Silvio Berlusconi Editore S.P.A. • Italy • **1988**

Tutto Musica & Spettacolo • Silvio Berlusconi Editore S.P.A. • Italy

VENNE POI IL MOMENTO PER UNA NUOVA AV-VENTURA. UN AMERICANO DI NOME AL BRODAX PRODUSSE UN FILM A CARTONI ANIMATI, "YELLOW SUBMARINE"...

AGLI STESSI BEATLES PIACQUE MOLTO IL PRODOTTO E ACCONSENTIRONO AD APPA-RIRE DAL VIVO ALLA FINE DEL FILM.

COSA DIRE SUI BIECHI BLU, GRANDI!

È PROPRIO PSICHEDELICO!

IL FILM RIMANE UN GROSSO SUCCESSO, SEBBE-NE I BEATLES NE SIANO STATI COINVOLTI SOLO IN MINIMA PARTE. CERTAMENTE STAVANO AN-DANDO INCONTRO AD UN'ALTRA CRISI...

LE SESSIONS DI RE-GISTRAZIONE MI FAN-NO SENTIRE GIÙ. PAUL CRITICA SEMPRE IL MIO STILE ALLA BATTERIA. TAL-VOLTA VORREI PIAN-TARE TUTTO

ANCORA PIÙ IMPORTANTE, UNA QUINTA PERSO-NALITÀ ERA ENTRATA NEL LORO RISTRETTISSIMO CIRCOLO. IL SUO NOME ERA YOKO ONO...

ANARCHY IN THE UK

Psychopathic aristocrats with Nazi leanings, an ultra-Marxist teenage skinhead indoctrinated by tabloid newspapers and a paparazzo involved in mad adventures are some of the characters found in *Brain Damage*, one of the most interesting British satirical magazines, brought out by Galaxy Publications—later Tristar Publications—from 1982 to 1992. Heavily politicized and anti-Thatcherite, the magazine set out to emulate the style of *Viz*, the popular comic magazine that commenced publication in 1979, mixing crude and hard-hitting language with stories that are often violent and have a high sexual content. On *Brain Damage*, characterized by a visceral aversion for the British establishment, worked some of the best cartoonists and illustrators, like Anthony Smith, Hunt Emerson and Kef F. Sutherland. Essentially each issue of *Brain Damage* turned around a central theme recounted through cartoons and strips, while the cover often portrayed a mascot that resembled the TV puppet Gilbert the Alien, a children's favourite in the eighties.

John Flores • Lucy in the Sky with Diamonds • USA • 2008

Andrea Rovati • Italy • **2007**

THE
BEATL

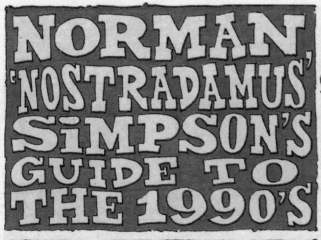

1991—2000

From the first "Coloquio internacional sobre la trascendencia de la obra de los Beatles" (Havana, November 1996) to the Parque John Lennon, opened by Fidel Castro on 8 December 2000 in Vedado, a neighbourhood of the Caribbean capital: change was in the air. It was a revolution with respect to what had gone before. At the outset, in fact, the Fab Four had not met with much favour among the more orthodox and rigid functionaries of the party, who did "not appreciate cer-

ONE DAY AT A TIME...

tain capitalist eccentricities." And so, while there were no actual anti-Beatles laws or rules, an "indirect and precautionary censorship" was imposed, as Ernesto Juan Castellano recalls in *Los Beatles en Cuba*. In the same decade, a beautiful comic-strip story with a journalistic slant came out in South Africa. Years earlier, despite allowing the release of the band's discs, the apartheid government had not exactly jumped for joy over some of the four's declarations.

the Beatles 1991–2000

1991

25 January. Acoustic performance by Paul McCartney who, from London, inaugurates the MTV series "Unplugged": the programme is broadcast on 3 April, and the CD is released a month later.

27 June. In Liverpool Cathedral, the Royal Liverpool Philharmonic Orchestra performs a composition of classical music by McCartney, the *Liverpool Oratorio*. On 18 November it is performed at Carnegie Hall in New York. In December the disc will go to the top of the Billboard classical charts, overtaking the album of the three tenors, Carreras, Domingo and Pavarotti.

13 November. The video *The First U.S. Visit* with archive footage of The Beatles appearances on *The Ed Sullivan Show* goes on sale.

December. The American sales of The Beatles' discs are certified, and celebrated: *Abbey Road* has sold 9 million copies, *The Beatles* 7 million, *1962–1966* and *1967–1970* 5 million each.

1992

24 July. Ringo Starr's European tour closes at the Foro Italico in Rome.

16 October. George Harrison takes part in the Bob Dylan 30th Anniversary Concert Celebration at Madison Square Garden in New York, where he sings "It's Not for You," "Absolutely Sweet Marie" and, in the collective grand finale, "My Back Pages."

November. An interactive version of the film *A Hard Day's Night*, on CD-ROM, is produced for the US market.

1993

5 March. Paul's world tour starts from Perth in Australia: 51,000 tickets have been sold in October.

16 April. McCartney headlines the Earth Day concert at the Hollywood Bowl: he will be joined on stage by Ringo to perform "Hey Jude."

2 October. The two collections, red and blue, *1962–1966* and *1967–1970* come out on CD.

November. The double album *Paul Is Live!* is published.

1994

19 January. Paul inducts Lennon into the Rock and Roll Hall of Fame at the annual ceremony held at the Waldorf Astoria in New York, with these words: "The thing you must remember is that I'm the number one John Lennon fan."

22 February. The album that Paul has recorded with Youth of Killing Joke under the name The Fireman is released in the US too.

May. Harrison's HandMade Films is sold to a Canadian company, Paragon, for 8.5 million dollars.

15 September. At a Sotheby's auction EMI buys for 78,500 pounds a tape belonging to a retired policeman, Bob Molyneux, containing two songs by Lennon's group The Quarrymen, "Puttin' on the Style" and "Baby Let's Play House," recorded on 6 July 1957.

November. Paul appears on TV, in the guise of a Shakespearian actor, in a spot to promote the Liverpool Institute for Performing Arts.

30 November. The double CD *The Beatles Live at the BBC* is released, with fifty-six performances broadcast on the radio between 1962 and 1965.

30 December. Ringo's former wife Maureen dies.

1995

28 January. Paul and Linda McCartney join up with Yoko to record "Hiroshima Sky Is Always Blue" at their studio in Sussex.

April. Release of *Come Together: America Salutes The Beatles*, an album of covers of Beatles songs by country music artists. There is a drawing by John Lennon on the cover.

23 April. *The Sunday Times* reveals that a Mr Peter Hodgson has found a tape recorded in 1959, with sixteen songs by The Quarrymen, in his attic.

12 June. Stella McCartney presents her fashion collection, for which her father has written a song, "Stella May."

4 September. Under the false name of the group Smokin' Mojo Filters, McCartney records "Come Together" with Paul Weller, Noel Gallagher and other musicians for the benefit album *Help!*.

14 September. The autograph text of Paul's "Getting Better" is sold at auction by Sotheby's in London, for 249,000 pounds.

19 November. The American network ABC begins transmission of six hours of the documentary *The Beatles Anthology*, comprising film clips and interviews that had never been broadcast before as well as two unreleased performances, co-produced with Jeff Lynne, "Free as a Bird" and "Real Love." The programme will be seen in ninety-four countries. In the framework of the massive operation of restoration on which Paul, George and Ringo work with George Martin, three double CDs will also be brought out and snapped up by collectors.

9 December. *Anthology Volume 1* tops the American album charts with 855,000 copies sold in a week: it is the sixteenth disc of The Beatles to reach number one in the United States.

30 December. "Sir Paul McCartney": Queen Elizabeth knights Paul, along with the composer Andrew Lloyd Webber.

1997

7 September. Derek Taylor, long-time press officer and factotum of the work team that backed up The Beatles in the sixties, dies at his home in Suffolk.

15 September. Paul participates in the "Music for Montserrat" concert to raise funds for victims of the volcano: among the other artists who perform at the Royal Albert Hall in London are Sting, Clapton, Knopfler and Elton John.

19 November. Paul McCartney's symphonic poem *Standing Stone* has its first performance in the United States, at Carnegie Hall in New York. The première was in London, on 14 October.

1998

17 April. Linda Eastman, Paul's wife, dies of cancer in Tucson, Arizona.

8 June. The three surviving Beatles appear together for the first time for almost thirty years at the memorial ceremony in honour of Linda held at the church of St Martins-in-the-Fields in Trafalgar Square, London.

29 July. Paul McCartney's house-museum at 20 Forthlin Road, in Liverpool, is opened to the public: it is considered a national monument.

20 October. George Martin, at the age of seventy-two, brings out the album *In My Life*, with cover versions of Beatles songs by a variety of celebrities, including some unlikely ones, Goldie Hawn, Sean Connery, Céline Dion...

25–26 December. The BBC broadcasts *The Brian Epstein Story*, a two-and-a-half-hour documentary on the manager of The Beatles, who died in 1967. After winning the BAFTA Award, it will be broadcast in a shortened version in the US as well, on 19 September 1999. Paul comments: "If anyone was the fifth Beatle, it was Brian."

1999

12 February. The tour marking the tenth anniversary of the All-Starr Band starts from Atlantic City, in New Jersey. On the stage with Ringo are Jack Bruce, Todd Rundgren and Gary Brooker, among others.

15 March. Paul McCartney and George Martin are inducted into the Rock and Roll Hall of Fame. In the jam session that follows, Paul is joined by Billy Joel in a rendering of "Let It Be."

10 April. Charity performance at the Royal Albert Hall, with Paul and many friends, from George Michael to Tom Jones and Elvis Costello: "Here, There and Everywhere. A Concert for Linda."

30 August. The remastered version of *Yellow Submarine* is given a spectacular launch in Liverpool, attended by 300,000 people and with 150 bands playing the celebrated motif. CDs and DVDs go on sale on 18 September: the songs on the soundtrack, never released before, are now available. It is estimated that a million dollars has been spent on the re-release.

30 September. At an auction at Christie's John Lennon's manuscript of "I Am the Walrus" is sold for 129,000 dollars and George Harrison's Rickenbacker guitar for 92,000 dollars.

30 December. George and his wife Olivia are victims of an attack at their Friar Park home in England.

2000

1 August. The certifications of sales by The Beatles on the US market are made public: 113 million discs in total, with *The White Album* reaching 18 million, seventh on the charts of all time.

5 October. Publication of the book *The Beatles Anthology*, a work of great dedication, 368 pages, 340,000 words, 1,300 pictures. The first run is 300,000 copies: the volume soars to the top of the best-seller lists.

17 October. The white piano on which Lennon composed and played "Imagine" is on sale at an auction organized at the Hard Rock Cafe by Mick Fleetwood: it is bought by George Michael, for 2,100,000 dollars. The price gets it into the Guinness Book of Records as the most expensive Steinway piano of all time.

13 November. Release of *The Beatles 1*, a compilation of twenty-seven singles by The Beatles that topped the charts. It is another commercial triumph, reaching number one in the charts of twenty-eight countries and selling 12 million copies in the first three weeks. It is the fastest selling album in the history of the music industry. A website devoted to rare Beatles material is also launched.

17 November. The American TV channel ABC broadcasts *The Beatles Revolution*, a two-hour documentary that gains a high audience rating.

MANAUS EXPRESS

*"Caro Sergio,
gli Jivaros, famigerati cacciatori di teste, sono forse estinti? Oppure vivono in villaggi civilizzati?"* Massimo Capalbo, Acri (CS).
Massimo è recidivo. Infatti si è già conquistato la citazione su *Mister No 199*, uscito all'inizio di questo stesso mese. Si merita la citazione bis perché, come direbbe il principe De Curtis alias Totò, questa sua domanda "arriva a fagiuolo". La riedizione della classica storia di Mister No sugli Jivaros comincia infatti proprio nell'albo che avete tra le mani.
Vi confesserò il mio punto debole: in realtà io, tra gli Jivaros, non sono mai stato! Nel corso dei miei primi viaggi in Amazzonia, più di vent'anni fa, non potevo contare, per quella regione, su nessun appoggio di quelli necessari (a quei tempi) per avventurarsi in zone selvagge. Non conoscevo, insomma, nel territorio Jivaro, né guide, né missionari, né proprietari terrieri, né capitribù; conoscenze che invece sono riuscito a procurarmi (e mi sono state utilissime) per altre regioni, come quelle, da me molto amate e frequentate, dell'Orinoco, del Rio Negro, dello Xingú. Nell'ultimo decennio la situazione è mutata; andare tra gli Jivaros non è più un problema insormontabile. Il punto è il seguente: a che pro, andarci adesso? Ormai, purtroppo, i mitici Jivaros non sono più quelli.

Con l'apertura di nuove strade, la scoperta del petrolio, l'infiltrazione del turismo, la tribù che, fino a vent'anni or sono, era considerata il terrore della foresta (un po' la Sudamerica, per dirla ha fatto la fine di altre cosiddette "civilizzate": si è venduta alla sottocultura che imperversa ai margini della società occidentale. Baracche prefabbricate, radioline e jeans costituiscono l'immagine attuale del popolo Jivaro. Progresso? Forse. E forse gli Jivaros sono contenti così. Ma io, sinceramente, così non voglio vederli. Perciò tra gli Jivaros non andrò mai.
Mi accontenterò di guardare le *tsantzas* (le teste ridotte e mummificate) in mostra nel museo di Guayaquil, in Ecuador (il territorio Jivaro si trova tra l'Amazzonia peruviana e quella ecuadoriana). E rivedrò con malinconia gli avventurosi film girati tra gli Jivaros, negli anni Cinquanta, dal cineasta esploratore Lewis Cotlow, film che fanno parte della mia videoteca avventurosa.

Altra lettera. È di *Marcello Gelso* di Roma, onnivoro bonelliano che, oltre a Mister No, non si perde un numero di Tex, Zagor e compagnia bella. Mi suggerisce un'idea originale: quella di trasferire per un'avventura il nostro Jerry Drake nella *swinging London* degli anni Sessanta, quella dei Beatles e delle minigonne. Lì, probabilmente, Mister No si farebbe crescere i capelli, ascolterebbe *Twist and Shout* e *Satisfaction*, e lascerebbe il suo jazz per i Beatles e i Rolling Stones. L'atmosfera proposta da Marcello è divertente, ma credo che quella leggendaria Londra anni Sessanta sarebbe elettrizzante per uno di noi, costretti a vivere nell'Italietta anni Novanta, non certo per un Mister No, abituato alle emozioni violente e contrastanti della selvaggia Amazzonia.
Ad ogni modo, l'idea di Marcello va premiata. Così, in questa pagina vi offro Mister No che ascolta i Beatles, in un bel disegno di Michele Pepe.
Un caro saluto.

Sergio Bonelli

1963
SEPT-OCT

MUSIC RELEASES ▼

HEADLINES ▶ KENNEDY SIGNS NUCLEAR TEST BAN / BRITISH EMBASSY BURNED IN MALAYSIA / POPULAR FILMS INCLUDE HITCHCOCK'S THE BIRDS AND KUBRICK'S DOCTOR STRANGELOVE / DODGERS BEAT YANKEES IN WORLD SERIES.

EVENTS IN BEATLES' LIVES ▼

"MY BOYFRIEND'S BACK" THE ANGELS

•

"IF I HAD A HAMMER" TRINI LOPEZ

•

"HEAT WAVE" MARTHA & THE VANDELLAS

•

"SURFER GIRL" BEACH BOYS

•

"BUSTED" RAY CHARLES

•

"DON'T THINK TWICE, IT'S ALL RIGHT" BOB DYLAN

•

"MEAN WOMAN BLUES" ROY ORBISON

THE SUN
BEATLEMANIA!

READY STEADY

Daily HERALD
SEIGE OF THE BEATLES!

HIT PAR
1. SHE LOVES The Beatles
2.
3.

SEPT. 10 JOHN AND PAUL MEET ROLLING STONES' MANAGER ANDREW OLDHAM, ATTEND A STONES REHERSALS

SEPT. 16 JOHN AND CYNTHIA VACATION IN PARIS, GEORGE IN THE U.S. TO VISIT HIS SISTER, PAUL AND RINGO FLY TO GREECE

OCT. 4 THE BEATLES APPEAR ON "READY, STEADY, GO"

OCT. 5 MINI-TOUR OF SCOTLAND COMMENCES

OCTOBER "SHE LOVES YOU" REMAINS AT #1 IN ENGLAND EVENTUALLY SELLING ONE MILLION COPIES IN ENGLAND ALONE, AND REMAINS THE ALL-TIME BEST SELLING BRITISH SINGLE FOR FOURTEEN YEARS

OCT. 13 THEY APPEAR LIVE ON "SATURDAY NIGHT AT THE LONDON PALLADIUM," THE EXCITEMENT SURROUNDING THE EVENT PROMPTS THE FIRST COINING OF THE WORD: BEATLEMANIA

OCT. 31 UPON RETURNING FROM SWEDEN, THEY ARE GREETED BY HUNDREDS OF SCREAMING TEENAGERS, THIS PHENOMENON IS WITNESSED BY ED SULLIVAN

OCT. 29 BRIAN EPSTEIN WRAPS UP A FILM DEAL FOR THE GROUP

OCT. 23 THE BEATLES FLY TO SWEDEN FOR THEIR FIRST FOREIGN TOUR

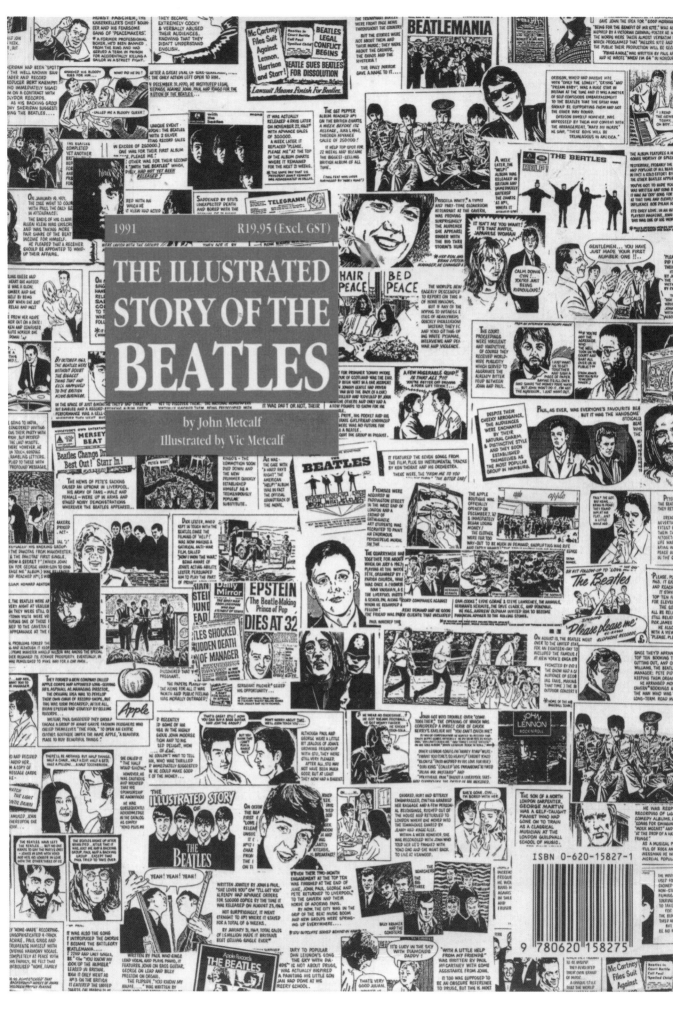

1991   R19.95 (Excl. GST)

THE ILLUSTRATED
STORY OF THE
BEATLES

by John Metcalf

Illustrated by Vic Metcalf

ISBN 0-620-15827-1

9 780620 158275

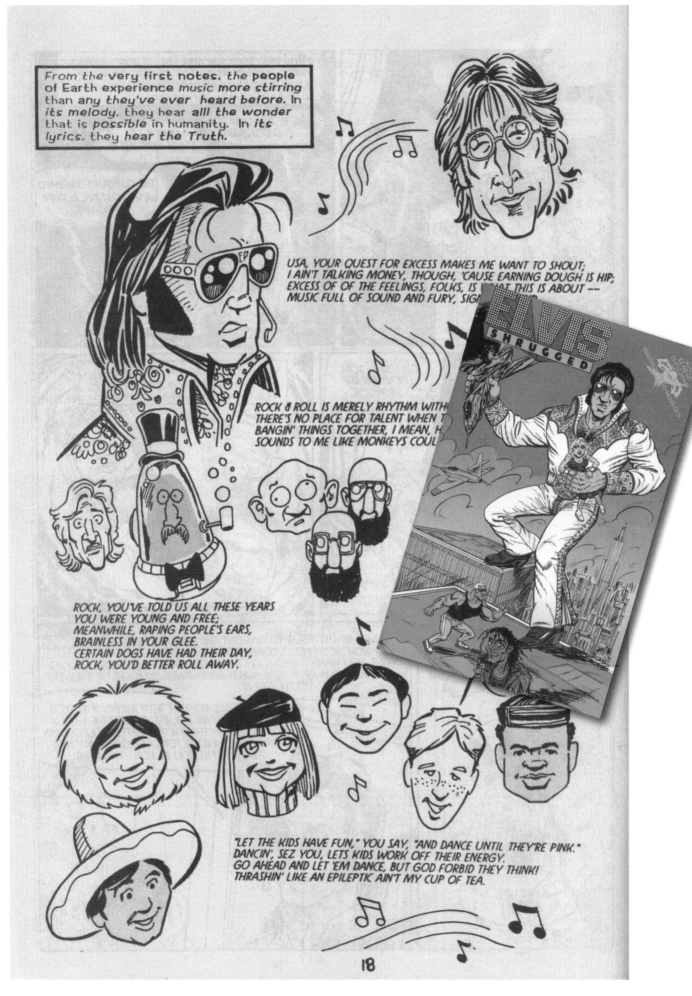

From the very first notes, the people of Earth experience *music more stirring* than any *they've ever heard before.* In *its melody,* they hear *alll the wonder* that is *possible* in humanity. In *its lyrics,* they hear the Truth.

USA, YOUR QUEST FOR EXCESS MAKES ME WANT TO SHOUT;
I AIN'T TALKING MONEY, THOUGH, 'CAUSE EARNING DOUGH IS HIP;
EXCESS OF OF THE FEELINGS, FOLKS, IS WHAT THIS IS ABOUT —
MUSIC FULL OF SOUND AND FURY, SIGN...

ROCK & ROLL IS MERELY RHYTHM WITH...
THERE'S NO PLACE FOR TALENT WHEN T...
BANGIN' THINGS TOGETHER, I MEAN, H...
SOUNDS TO ME LIKE MONKEYS COUL...

ROCK, YOU'VE TOLD US ALL THESE YEARS
YOU WERE YOUNG AND FREE;
MEANWHILE, RAPING PEOPLE'S EARS,
BRAINLESS IN YOUR GLEE.
CERTAIN DOGS HAVE HAD THEIR DAY,
ROCK, YOU'D BETTER ROLL AWAY.

"LET THE KIDS HAVE FUN," YOU SAY, "AND DANCE UNTIL THEY'RE PINK."
DANCIN', SEZ YOU, LETS KIDS WORK OFF THEIR ENERGY.
GO AHEAD AND LET 'EM DANCE, BUT GOD FORBID THEY THINK!
THRASHIN' LIKE AN EPILEPTIC AIN'T MY CUP OF TEA.

18

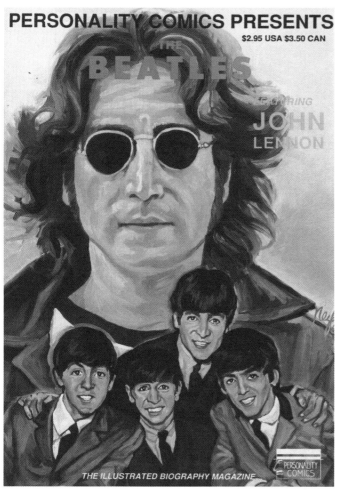

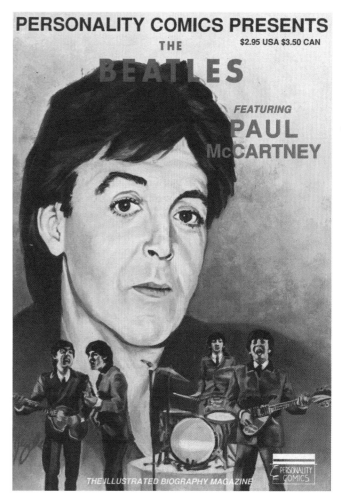

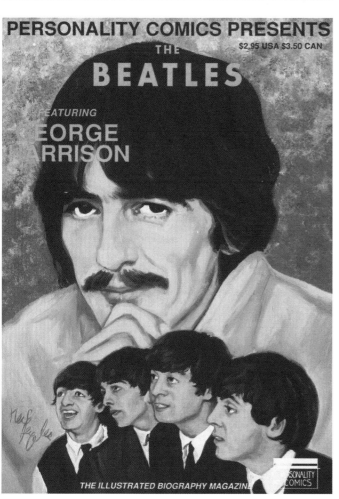

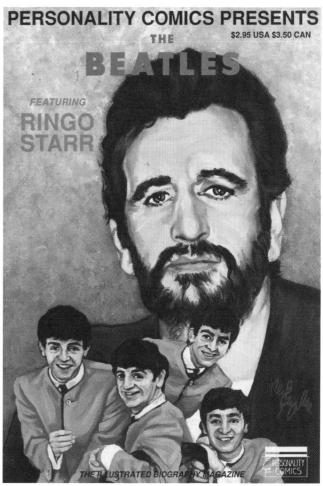

STRAWBERRY FIELDS FOREVER

Lorenzo Bartoli and Andrea Domestici, the duo who created the Italian humorous comic strip *Arthur King*, had read a lot of science fiction, and in particular Philip Dick. The story is simple. Arthur King and his father Orion design and build various kinds of robots and androids. The project gets out of control and the pair of scientists are faced with a series of problems, especially after Sandor III, the emperor of the known universe, uses their prototypes to begin construction of bio-mechanical war machines on a massive scale. Arthur does not like this and turns himself into a hunter of androids, cyborgs and an endless series of other pseudo-human creatures, helped by Rex, a baby tyrannosaur. In this continual hunt there is still time to meet John Lennon and walk in his strawberry fields, which in that devastated world of the future are even more incredible than the meeting with the musician himself.

GREEN ARROW 69. December, 1992. Published monthly by DC Comics Inc., 1325 Avenue of the Americas, New York, NY 10019. POSTMASTER: Send address changes to GREEN ARROW, DC Comics Subscriptions, P.O. Box 0528, Baldwin, NY 11510. Annual subscription rate $21.00. Canadian subscribers must add $8.00 for postage and GST. GST # is R125921072. All other foreign countries must add $12.00 for postage. U.S. funds only. Copyright © 1992 DC Comics Inc. All Rights Reserved. All characters featured in this issue, the distinctive likenesses thereof, and all related indicia are trademarks of DC Comics Inc. The stories, characters and incidents mentioned in this magazine are entirely fictional. For advertising space contact: Tom Ballou, (212) 636-5520. Printed on recyclable paper. Printed in Canada.
DC Comics Inc. A Warner Bros. Inc. Company

LE DUE SFERE MAGICHE, PADRONE!

PER UN A... POTRAI V... IMMAGI... FUT...

EHI, MA QUI SONO CON I BEATLES! E PAUL HA IN MANO UN DISCO D'ORO!(*)

(*)RICONOSCIMENTO DATO A CHI VENDE PIU' DI UN MILIONE DI DISCHI DI UNA STESSA CANZONE!

E QUI RICEVIAMO LA MEDAGLIA DELL'ORDINE DELL'IMPERO BRITANNICO! UAO!

DAVVERO LA REGINA MI NOMINERA' BARONETTO?

COSI' HAI LETTO NEL FUTURO E COSI' ACCADRA'!

LES CINQ «FAB FIVE»

SAF : *Et le nom des «Beatles»? Qui l'a trouvé, Mike?*

MICHEL : *(riant)* Je dois vous l'avouer, c'est moi. Au début, on s'appelait les «RMPGJ», c'était difficile à retenir! Un soir qu'on était dans un bar, je décide d'offrir une tournée aux gars. Alors, avec mon accent tout de travers, je dis au serveur : «Five beatles of beer, please»! Le nom est resté!

SAF : *Est-ce que les Beatles ont marché fort dès le début?*

MICHEL : Ah oui! Rien qu'à penser aux premiers shows, je viens la chair de poule sur la poitrine *(il se met à déboutonner sa chemise)*... Regarde!

SAF : Euh, ok, ça va...

MICHEL : Les groupies tombaient comme des mouches épileptiques. Il n'y en avait que pour nous. Mon stylo a fait

un burn-out tellement on signait d'autographes! On était véritablement agressés dans les rues! Même nos gardes du corps devaient avoir des gardes du corps! La Beatlemania, mon ami, c'était effrayant!

SAF : *Mais comment ça se fait qu'on ne te voit presque jamais sur les photos des Beatles?*

MICHEL : C'est simple : c'était toujours moi qui prenais les photos pour la gang. Les gars insistaient toujours pour que je prenne les photos. Ils disaient que j'étais le meilleur photographe! Des vrais chums, tu vois!

SAF : *C'est la seule raison? Est-ce que les gars ne voulaient pas un peu te laisser dans l'ombre, mon Michou?*

MICHEL : *(soupirant)* Peut-être un peu... Écoute, dans les premières années, avant qu'on soit super connus, il y a eu des

> PAUL ET JOHN ONT ÉCRIT LA CHANSON «MICHELLE MA BELLE» JUSTE POUR M'AGACER PARCE QUE J'AIMAIS PARFOIS ME DÉGUISER EN FEMME!

Photo : Allô-Vedettes

frictions. Paul et moi, on est des leaders naturels, tu sais, et on avait nos divergences musicales. Ainsi, il insistait pour que je ne chante pas et éliminait le gazou de la plupart des chansons en spectacle. Mon rôle se limitait souvent à frapper dans les mains et tenir le rythme. Je pense que Paul était un peu jaloux de moi.

New York. Nous descendons de l'avion en février 1964. C'est la folie furieuse. Un serrement de coeur me vient à l'esprit quand j'y repense! J'ai dû me dépêcher pour rejoindre les gars... les sièges 3e classe sont dans la queue de l'avion!

Photo : Keystone et Allô Vedettes

SAF 74 15

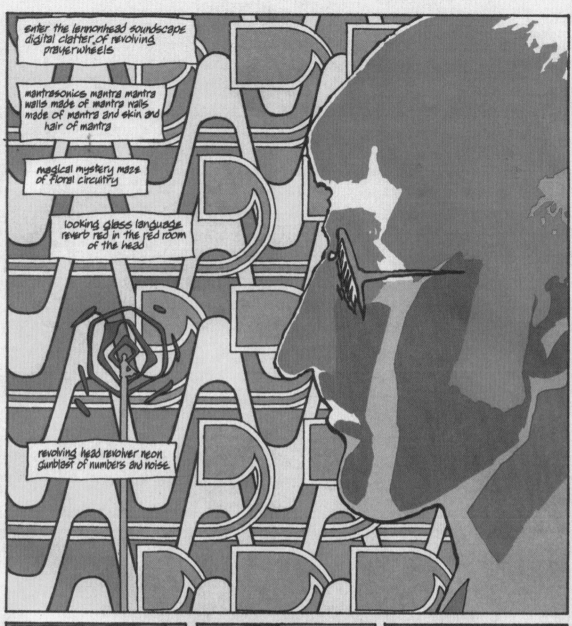

enter the lennonhead soundscape digital clatter of revolving prayerwheels

mantrasonics mantra mantra walls made of mantra walls made of mantra and skin and hair of mantra

magical mystery maze of floral circuitry

looking glass language reverb red in the red room of the head

revolving head revolver neon gunblast of numbers and noise

fizzing sherbetstorms of light particles

bumper tilt eggman hologram blizzard

the head the oracle head speaks in rhyming sounds hammerchime fuzztone piano

let me take you down down

say the word

it is not dying

be reborn be light go and come again

rise from the grave of himself

bonny jock lennon is did and goon

it is not dying

the boy born again beautiful boy beautiful boy

it is not dying

CHAS SAID HE HAD A PLAN. WE WERE GOIN' FOR BROKE. IF IT WORKED I'D BE A BIG STAR — FAST. IF NOT, WE'D BOTH JUST BE BROKE.

Dear Dad,
I'm in England, Dad. I met some people and they're going to make me a big star. We changed my name to J-I-M-I.

THE IDEA WAS FOR ME TO PLAY AROUND AS MUCH AS POSSIBLE AND GET HEARD BY THE "RIGHT" PEOPLE — THE GUYS WHO LET THE REST OF THE WORLD KNOW WHAT'S HAPPENIN'. THAT WAY WE COULD BE "DISCOVERED," SORT OF MAKE IT UP FROM THE "UNDERGROUND." CHAS ARRANGED FOR ME TO START JAMMING RIGHT AWAY AROUND THE VARIOUS CLUBS — BLAISES, LES COUSINS, POLYTECHNIC OF CENTRAL LONDON AND SCOTCH OF SAINT JAMES. HE KNEW JUST ABOUT EVERYBODY — JEFF BECK, ERIC CLAPTON, PETE TOWNSHEND, PAUL McCARTNEY, JOHN LENNON, MICK JAGGER, BRIAN JONES — *EVERYBODY!* ... THEY ALL SHOWED UP TO CHECK ME OUT...

WAKE UP TO THE SOUND OF MUSIC

After the success of *Madman*, Michael Dalton "Mike" Allred, one of the finest comic-strip artists in America, decided to create a comic whose guiding thread would be music, one of his passions. In addition to being a filmmaker and a former TV reporter, Mike is in fact also the leader of the rock band The Gear. And so *Red Rocket 7* was born, a history of rock & roll from 1950 until 1998 told from the point of view of an alien, friend of the most important musicians, battling against other aliens whose attitude towards music is similar to that of the Blue Meanies in *Yellow Submarine*. Everything will turn out well because, when all is said and done, "music is one of the elements of our existence, perhaps one of the most important, capable of making men so delightfully crazy and creative and life more intense" (Friedrich Nietzsche).

Arthur King. La precedenza al mito • no. 20 • Macchia Nera S.R.L. • Italy • **1996**

172

DURANTE LA COMIDA ME PIDIERON QUE CANTA-RA LA CANCION Y NO SOLO CANTE SI NO QUE AL PREGUNTARME POR MIS PROYECTOS LES CONTE MI PROXIMO COMIX SOBRE UNOS HOMBRECILLOS LLAMADOS BLUE MINNIES QUE HABITABAN EN EL PAIS DE LA PIMIENTA.

LO UNICO QUE RECUERDO SON SUS CARAS MIENTRAS FINALIZABA MI HISTORIA Y...

AMID THE UNCERTAINTY OF A WORLD BENT ON SELF DESTRUCTION, OUTRAGED YOUTH FINDS A VOICE IN ROCK 'N' ROLL.

PARENTS QUICKLY PROCLAIM IT TO BE THE WORK OF THE DEVIL, AND BLAME IT FOR THE DOWNFALL OF A GENERATION...

COMIC STRIP IN CANADA IS CALLED "BANDE DESSINÉE"

Founded in 1987, *Safarir*, a transliteration of *Ça fait rire* ("It Makes You Laugh"), is one of the many satirical magazines in French that are published in Canada, a nation that has a long and varied tradition, although a little-known one, of comic strips, divided equally between its two linguistic communities. Unlike other publications, the one created by Sylvain Bolduc and Michel Morin was aimed essentially at teenage readers and had a style similar to that of *Mad*, with comic strips, parodies of US films and Canadian TV programmes and an eye to events and people in the news, including, for example, The Beatles. Cameos and citations apart, number 74 of 1994 is an issue devoted almost entirely to a hypothetical reunion of the quartet: on the cover, a John Lennon revenant who looms over his surviving colleagues with crooked glasses and a look straight out of *Pet Sematary*.

Ese mediodía del 6 de julio, el verano reina en Liverpool. La ciudad portuaria sufre los embates de la excepcional ola de calor que hace una docena de días que atenaza a toda Europa. Este sábado, al alba, la población ha huido del centro de la ciudad buscando el aire más fresco de las orillas del Mersey.

Tras llegar de Londres en el primer tren directo, Mortimer sale de la estación.

¡A Woolton, por favor! ¡Rápido!

El taxi arranca enseguida en dirección al sur de la ciudad.

Veinte minutos después, se detiene ante St. Peter's Church, a donde ha acudido una alegre multitud a participar en la fiesta parroquial anual.

Preguntándose cómo podrá encontrar a su hombre entre la multitud, Mortimer saca una entrada...

Tenga los 6 peniques.

Thank you, sir, ¡que se divierta!

...y se dirige al centro de las festividades del día...

...organizadas en una vasta extensión de césped detrás de la iglesia.

"Come, little darling, come and go with me!"

¡Perdone, muchacho! Busco al rector de St. Peter. ¿Sabe dónde puedo encontrarlo?

Lo siento, señor. ¡Soy de Allerton y no conozco a nadie de aquí!

Espera, Paul. Yo conozco al reverendo Pryce Jones, señor. Acabo de verlo por allí...

Déjeme un momento... ¡Allí abajo! A la derecha del escenario.

14

2001–2010

The Church has always had a different conception of time. And so, forty years after The Beatles' break-up, *L'Osservatore Romano*, the newspaper of the Holy See, while recalling their dissolute life, reappraised the group in the name of the beauty of its music. This posthumous celebration provoked a caustic response from Ringo Starr: "Didn't the Vatican say we were satanic or possibly satanic—and they've still forgiven us? I think the Vatican, they've got more to talk about than The Beatles." The lack of affection on the part of

AND IN THE END...

the upper echelons of the Catholic Church was provoked not only by the musical and generational values represented by the four in the sixties, but also by John Lennon's celebrated remark about the Beatles and Jesus in 1966, often taken out of its context. After forty-four years the *Osservatore* considered those words nothing more than "bragging by a young English working-class musician who had [...] enjoyed unexpected success and was struggling to cope with it." Hallelujah.

the Beatles 2001–2010

2001

27 March. The wooden stage in St Peter's Church Hall, at Woolton, where John and Paul had first met forty-four years earlier, has to be dismantled to allow modernization of the building. This provokes a controversy and angry letters from fans, as well as the intervention of Liverpool town council, who suggest putting the stage up for auction. On 27 November, however, the attempt to sell the whole thing for 50,000 pounds fails. The stage will nevertheless be saved.

29 June. It is officially declared that in 2002, when the work of construction of the city's new hub is finished, Liverpool airport will be named after John Lennon, with a logo featuring his self-portrait and the words "above us only sky" taken from his song "Imagine."

9 July. A series of alarming reports come out on the health of George Harrison, who is suffering from cancer: in May he had undergone an operation in the United States, and now there is news of another one at San Giovanni Hospital in Bellinzona, Switzerland.

24 August. The architect John Tweedie announces that in a couple of years a unique hotel will be opened in Castle Street, in the heart of Liverpool, with extensive references to The Beatles. To be called A Hard Day's Night, it will be connected with the premises of the Cavern and has obtained the approval of Paul, George and Ringo.

20 September. Dougie Millings, the tailor who made the classic collarless suits with which The Beatles were launched in 1963, dies at the age of eighty-eight: his creations can also be seen on the covers of some of McCartney's later albums, *Wild Life*, 1971, and *Band on the Run*, 1973.

7 November. From Staten Island University Hospital, in New York, comes the news that George's condition is deteriorating. Paul and Ringo will go to see him on 21 November.

29 November. George Harrison dies in Los Angeles, at the age of fifty-eight. His wife Olivia and son Dhani are with him to the end. His body will be cremated at a ceremony organized by his Hare Krishna friends. His death receives enormous attention in the international media and among his fellow musicians.

28 December. *I Am Sam*, a film starring Sean Penn and filled with references to the Beatles, arrives in American cinemas: for the soundtrack, instead of the original songs of The Beatles, for which over 4 million dollars are requested for the rights, the director uses a series of cover versions by The Black Crowes, Ben Harper, Eddie Vedder, Rufus Wainwright, Sheryl Crow, The Wallflowers...

2002

8 February. Bob Wooler, DJ at the Cavern, where The Beatles performed about four hundred times between 1961 and 1963, dies in Liverpool at the age of seventy-six. On 4 March Herbert Hughes, one of the official photographers of the early days, also passes away.

16 May. The exhibition *The Quarrymen and Skiffle. The UK Years* opens at the Beatles Story Museum in Liverpool. Among the objects on display, the banjo played at the time by John Lennon.

18 May. From the figures given in the Guinness Book of Hit Singles the author David Roberts concludes that Liverpool is the capital of pop music, the source of its greatest successes: he has calculated that 6% of chart-topping records are by artists from the city, with The Beatles obviously in pole position.

30 May. Julian Lennon announces that the official website of the Liverpool Lennons, dedicated to the history of the family from the nineteenth century to the present day, is on line.

3 June. Grand concert for Queen Elizabeth's Golden Jubilee: on the fiftieth anniversary of her accession to the throne (1952), twelve thousand lucky people are admitted to the grounds of Buckingham Palace, while almost a million watch the performances on giant screens in the Mall. Among the many artists, Paul McCartney plays several numbers, including "While My Guitar Gently Weeps" in a duet with Eric Clapton.

11 June. Paul marries the thirty-four-year-old Heather Mills in a seventeenth-century Irish church. The best man is his brother Mike, who played the same role at his wedding with Linda.

25 July. Queen Elizabeth attends the opening of the new airport in Liverpool named after Lennon and visits the city's Walker Art Gallery where an exhibition of McCartney pictures is being held.

23 September. A deluxe DVD edition of the film *A Hard Day's Night* is published: it contains various bonus features.

2 October. George Martin presents his autobiography *Playback* in Melbourne. It is a limited edition of only two thousand copies: it includes many rare pictures and documents and a CD, all for the price of 880 dollars.

19 November. *Brainwashed*, George Harrison's posthumous album, comes out: there are eleven new songs, for which the final selection and production are done by his son Dhani and friend Jeff Lynne.

29 November. On the first anniversary of his death, a concert-tribute for George is held at the Royal Albert Hall: the performers include Paul, Ringo, Billy Preston, Eric Clapton and Ravi Shankar.

8 December. Among the various records assigned to the Beatles in the annual edition of the Guinness Book, that of having sold over a billion discs in forty years.

2003

10 January. About five hundred tapes, lasting 16 minutes each, made during the "Get Back Sessions" related to the preparation of *Let It Be*, are recovered by investigators after EMI is required to pay 600,000 dollars compensation for the stolen recordings.

23 February. The Beatles' sound engineer Geoff Emerick, who had already received a Grammy for his work on the albums *Revolver*, *Sgt. Pepper's* and *Abbey Road*, receives the prestigious award for lifetime achievement.

25 February. To celebrate the anniversary of George's birth, the Beatles Story Museum puts on display his first guitar, an Egmond bought for 4 pounds.

25 March. Release of *Ringo Rama*, Ringo Starr's new album which contains a song in memory of George, "Never Without You." The DVD of the limited edition includes appearances by Clapton, David Gilmour, Willie Nelson...

31 March. *The Beatles Anthology* comes out on DVD. The ten-hour documentary is on the first four discs, while the fifth DVD has 81 minutes of archive material, with sessions never released before.

4 April. Paul McCartney's company MPL buys the copyright to twenty-three songs by Carl Perkins, one of the fathers of rock & roll.

10 May. Paul plays for a select audience of a few hundred people at the Colosseum: the tickets cost a thousand dollars and the proceeds go to supporting archaeological initiatives for Rome. The day after he stages a free concert for around half a million fans at the Imperial Fora.

24 May. Paul plays in Moscow's Red Square. Three days earlier he had received an honorary degree from the St Petersburg Conservatory.

24 September. The documentary of the tribute concert to George Harrison is presented at the Warner Bros. Studios in Los Angeles: Paul, Ringo, Yoko Ono and Olivia and Dhani Harrison attend.

18 November. Release of *Let It Be... Naked*, i.e. the version of The Beatles's album as Paul McCartney originally intended it: it had subsequently been modified, distorted according to some, by Phil Spector's mixing and production.

2004

31 January. The magazine *Rolling Stone* publishes a list of the five hundred best albums in history (in the view of the editors): The Beatles have four titles in the top ten.

7 May. The London auction house Christie's offers the copy of the contract between The Beatles and Brian Epstein signed on 1 October 1962. It is sold for the equivalent of 180,660 euros.

19 June. Shortly after his sixty-second birthday, Paul holds the three thousandth concert of his career in Russia, at St Petersburg, where he performs for the first time.

16 November. New version, twenty years later, of the 1984 benefit song "Do They Know It's Christmas?" The initiative comes from the original two promoters, Bob Geldof and Midge Ure: the only performers from the 1984 disc, which sold over 50 million copies, are Bono and Paul McCartney, on bass.

2005

28–29 January. Around twenty Italian bands specializing in covers of The Beatles come together at the Abbey Road Studios: Quarrymen, Apple Pies, Beatalks, Beattops, Two of Us and others record a double album for the Beatlesiani d'Italia Associati.

2 July. The audience for the "Live 8" concert, staged in ten of the world's cities to combat hunger and poverty in Africa, is estimated at two billion. Paul McCartney performs in London and in September will take part in another initiative of solidarity, "ReAct Now: Music and Relief," in support of the victims of Hurricane Katrina, in Louisiana.

5 July. The annual *Book of British Hit Singles*, the official record of sales in Great Britain, comes out. Queen come out on top, with 1322 weeks in the charts; The Beatles are in second place, with 1293.

5 August. In a poll held by the magazine *Uncut* asking people to name the events in the world of entertainment that have changed our history, The Beatles are in third place, with "She Loves You."

8 December. On the 25th anniversary of his death, a large crowd gathers in Central Park to commemorate John Lennon. In the meantime *The Times* reveals that the artist had been working on a plan for the reunion of The Beatles to make a record.

2006

February. Paul receives three nominations at the Grammy Awards, for the album *Chaos and Creation: in the Back Yard*.

8 May. Third sentence in twenty years on the dispute between The Beatles and Steve Jobs over the Apple brand name. The court in London gives the American company the right to use the apple symbol in advertising for the iPod. In 1991 The Beatles had won the case and been awarded 26 million dollars.

6 June. Billy Preston dies in Arizona, at the age of fifty-nine: he had collaborated with The Beatles on many albums, from *Abbey Road* to *Let It Be*.

25 September. Paul's fourth album of "classical" music: *Ecce Cor Deum*.

20 November. Release of the album *Love*, with several new versions of Beatles songs, remixed by George Martin and his son Giles. The occasion is provided by the hit musical that the Canadian theatre company Le Cirque du Soleil has been staging in Las Vegas since June.

2007

4 June. Paul's fortieth post-Beatles album, *Memory Almost Full*, is the first to come out under the new Hear Music label, owned by the Starbucks group.

1 August. The round glasses with a gold frame that John Lennon wore during The Beatles' concerts at the Budokan in Tokyo, in 1966, are sold at auction for about 1,500,000 pounds.

8 October. In a BBC poll Paul McCartney's "Ebony and Ivory" duet with Stevie Wonder is voted the Worst of All Time; at the top of the Ten Best Duets is Sinead O'Connor and The Chieftains with their "Foggy Dew."

12 October. Release of the film *Across the Universe* by the director Julie Taymor, centred on the song of the same name by The Beatles: music is put to brilliant use to tell the story, with reinterpretations of around thirty songs by the Fab Four. Cameos for Bono and Joe Cocker.

8 December. *Arrivano i Beatles. Storie di una generazione*, the largest exhibition on The Beatles ever staged outside Britain, opens at Aosta in Italy, split between the Archaeological Museum and the St Benin Centre.

2008

18 February. Paul and Heather Mills get divorced after a bitter legal dispute over the "settlement" demanded by his wife.

16 June. In Milan the exhibition *Beatles '68* opens, devoted to the relationship between the Fab Four and that crucial year for the future of society and youth culture.

6 November. Paul receives the Ultimate Legend award from MTV Europe at a ceremony in Liverpool.

20 October. Release of *All Together Now*, the DVD that documents the making and the backstage of the Cirque du Soleil's musical *Love*. The film, 86 minutes long, is dedicated to Neil Aspinall, one of The Beatles' principal collaborators, at the head of Apple Corps, who had died on 24 March.

24 November. Under the pseudonym The Fireman, Paul releases the album *Electric Arguments*, recorded in his Sussex studio in just two weeks.

2009

4 March. Liverpool Hope University institutes a master's degree in "Songs of The Beatles": thirty students, a twelve-week course and a fee of 3400 pounds to sustain the interest in The Beatles from the university viewpoint as well. An interest which brings 300,000 visitors to the Cavern every year. "At least eight thousand books on The Beatles have been published," they say at the vice-chancellor's office, "but there has not been one academic study."

4 April. Paul headlines the concert at Radio City Music Hall in New York for the David Lynch Foundation: one of the guests is Ringo Starr, with whom he performs "With a Little Help from My Friends."

9 September. The videogame *The Beatles: Rock Game* and remastered versions of their official albums go on sale.

2010

13 April. An article rehabilitating The Beatles after almost forty years appears in *L'Osservatore Romano*. Asked for a comment, Ringo Starr's response can be boiled down to: "who gives a damn."

2 June. During the ceremony for the award of the Gershwin Prize at the White House, Paul sings "Michelle" before President Obama and his wife Michelle. The evening concludes with a choral rendering of "Hey Jude."

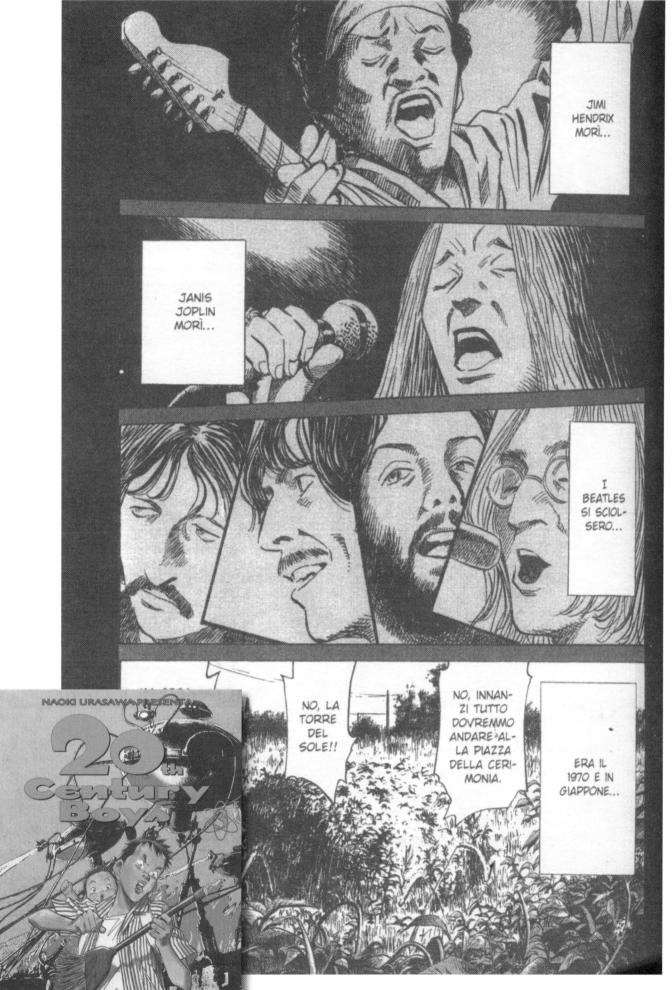

Le Petit Beatles Illustré • by Germani, Jean Preux, Jean-Bernard Boulnois • Source Publishing Genève, La Sirène • Switzerland • **2001**

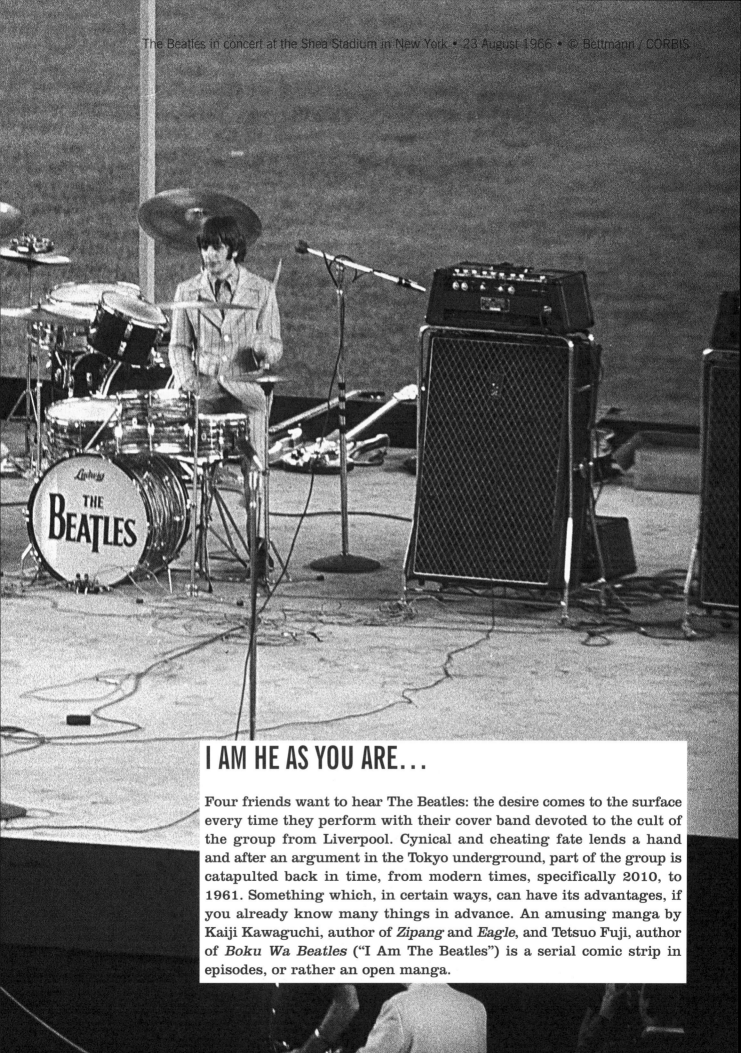

I AM HE AS YOU ARE…

Four friends want to hear The Beatles: the desire comes to the surface every time they perform with their cover band devoted to the cult of the group from Liverpool. Cynical and cheating fate lends a hand and after an argument in the Tokyo underground, part of the group is catapulted back in time, from modern times, specifically 2010, to 1961. Something which, in certain ways, can have its advantages, if you already know many things in advance. An amusing manga by Kaiji Kawaguchi, author of *Zipang* and *Eagle*, and Tetsuo Fuji, author of *Boku Wa Beatles* ("I Am The Beatles") is a serial comic strip in episodes, or rather an open manga.

Forever Maelstrom • no. 1 • DC Comics • USA • **2003**

Where did you go?
Where do I go?
When I lost you I lost all my dreams
You won't believe what it's done to me
No one could do as well as you
And look what happened
What's the use?

Where did you go?
Where do I go?
When I lost you I lost happiness
No more hope for my loneliness
No day goes by that I don't cry
For what I lost
That winter night.

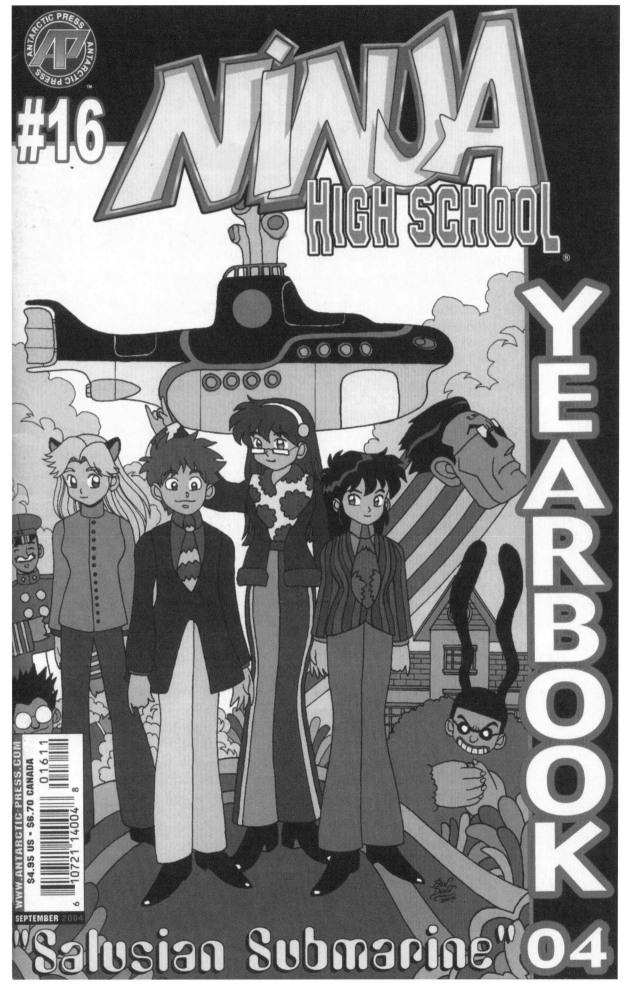

Il Trattore Giallo

Contis e filistocjis par une flabe musicâl dai Beât Lès

Racconti e filastrocche per una fiaba musicale dei Beât Lès

une storie furlane di Alberto Zeppieri

cui pipins *disegni* di Andrea (Dree) Venier

musiche dai

BEÂT LÈS

Zuan, Pauli, Zorç e Rico

NUMAR UN
difindìn e difondìn il furlan!

Associazion Culturâl

Miluç

Mission Team

SHE CAME ALONG TO TURN ON EVERYONE...

The Beatles were always surrounded by young and beautiful women, ready to fall at their feet. With one, however, the opposite happened. Impossible? Absolutely not, given that she was Little Annie Fanny, protagonist of the comic strip of the same name by Harvey Kurtzman—inventor of *Mad*—and Will Elder. Right from her first appearance (*Playboy*, October 1962), Little Annie Fanny proved an incredible success. In each adventure the blonde, curvaceous and provocative Annie ended up naked, pursued by swarms of horny men. And the stories delighted in being politically incorrect, often featuring celebrities. So The Beatles could not fail to put in an appearance and, in the issue of December 1965, encounter her in *Annie Meets the Bleatles*—with the name of the group deliberately mangled—in a story in pure slapstick comedy style. As usual, our heroine ends up with bare breasts and an astonished expression. The same thing happens in *Little Annie in India*, where she is transported to Maharishi Mahesh Yogi's ashram in Rishikesh. It goes without saying that for John, Paul, George and Ringo meditation becomes as important as beefsteak to a vegetarian.

The actress Tracy Reed in a photograph published in *Playboy* • 1963 • © Bob Penn / CONTRASTO

Diamantes en el paraíso

Un encuentro imaginario entre John Lennon & George Harrison

Rodolfo R. Vázquez
Guinness World Record

Gárgola
ediciones

...against stiff opposition in this, the *Golden Age* of Music Hall.

The Victoria Hall, The People's Palace, The Wear Music Hall – "the largest and most magnificent in Europe" - and *The Avenue Theatre*, hosting Houdini, all vie for attention.

Henry Irving, the greatest actor of his time, makes his first professional stage appearance at *The Lyceum*, Lambton Street in 1856. *Buffalo Bill's Wild West Show* and Blondin the tightrope walker draw the crowds at outdoor venues. Tough acts to follow but its rivals are long gone and The Empire remains.

They've all played this theatre, you know...

Stan Laurel, born in Lancashire and raised just north of Sunderland, writes and performs a sketch here in 1908: *Home from the Honeymoon*, later made into the film *Another Fine Mess*. He returns with Oliver Hardy in the 1950s.

Charlie Chaplin, Marie Lloyd, Harry Lauder, Chico Marx, W.C. Fields - billed as "eccentric juggler" - they've all trod these boards.

From Benny Hill to Marlene Dietrich, from Yehudi Menuhin to *The Shadows* (who record an instrumental in 1965 entitled *Alice in Sunderland*) to Lancashire band The Beatles; a prodigious litany of famous actors and show business stars...

13

Le Mersey Beat
à Hambourg

Dessins de Vox

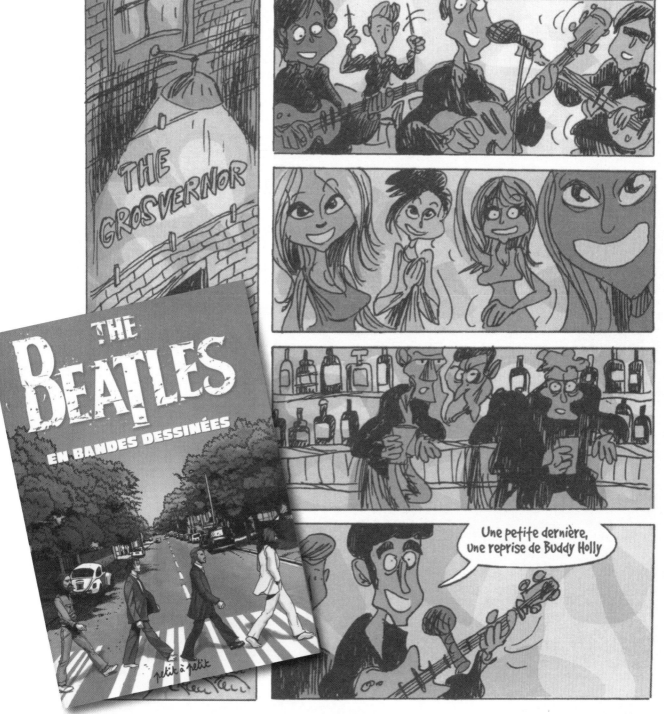

ALL YOU NEED IS...

England has always been an ideal place in which to set stories of terror and horror. Perfect, then, if there are vampires involved as well. This is what happens in Ricketts and Farritor's graphic novel *Night Trippers*. In a London at the height of the swinging sixties some strange deaths occur, the work of Count Dracula and his acolytes who meet up in the traditional lonely manor house, somewhere in the countryside. Their devotion to the Lord of Evil is based on a highly epicurean and capitalist creed: success, power, money and eternal youth. Their antagonists are a couple of octogenarian patients in a hospital, hunters of vampires by night, and a teddy boy Elvis fanatic who speaks in a Lenny Bruce style of beatnik slang and falls in love with the young heroine, who is a victim of the count's malevolent designs. In the background The Beatles murmur "All You Need Is Blood" and mix up magic and music. In the end good wins out and the count dies. In the meantime, in New York, a young artist called Andy Warhol takes part in a ceremony where he witnesses the resurrection of a nobleman from Eastern Europe...

[LA VIGNETTA]

TELESCHERNO

DI STEFANO DISEGNI

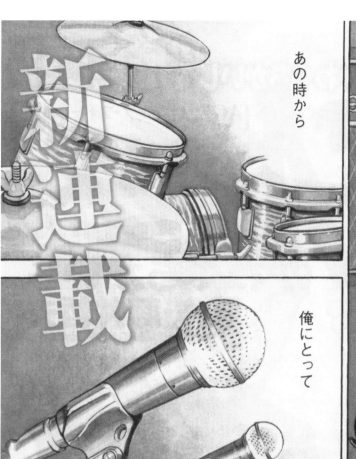

新連載

あの時から

俺にとって

親父のCDを
何気に聞いた
小学3年の夏

「リアル」
だった

ビートルズ
だけが

REVOLVER

THE FAB4

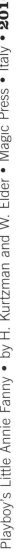

105

224

JOHN LENNON

If Lennon did not find it at all easy being John Lennon, then it comes as no surprise that it can be complicated to recount the death of a legend and avoid, at the same time, its celebration with prayers, incense and perfunctory tears. To do so through drawings is even more difficult. While *Johnny* is a series of more classical reminiscences, in *Hommage*, on the other hand, we find emotional crowds that, after the due sixty seconds of si-

I READ THE NEWS TODAY, OH BOY...

lence to commemorate the dead musician, immediately set up a bazaar for collectors with Winston Ono dolls made out of sugar, as in the irreverent story drawn by Margerin or in Giberat's John/Little Nemo, and in Matena's account poised between psychoanalysis and fantasy, with its surprise ending, without forgetting the historic narration of the Mexican and Argentinian comic or the Brazilian tribute, which is really Lennonesque.

John Lennon 1940–2010

1940

9 October. He is born in Liverpool to Julia Stanley and Alfred Lennon: the family, once called O'Leannain, has distant origins in the west of Ireland.

1956

20 June. His mother buys him a guitar by mail-order: it costs ten pounds.

1957

March. Inspired by Lonnie Donegan and skiffle, John founds his first group, The Blackjacks, with his school friend Pete Shotton.
24 May. Changing the name to The Quarrymen, they perform live for the first time.
9 June. The Quarrymen take part in a competition for young bands at the Empire Theatre, but do not pass the audition.
15 July. His mother is killed, run over by a car driven by an off-duty policeman while crossing the road. The loss will leave a deep mark on John's career.
18 October. Paul McCartney's first official performance with The Quarrymen: at the Conservative Club in Liverpool. John had also invited him to play on 7 August, for the group's debut at the Cavern Club, but Paul had not been able to come, as he had a previous engagement at a scout camp with his brother Michael.

1959

15 November. Lennon, McCartney and George Harrison, who had joined The Quarrymen the previous year, now call themselves Johnny and the Moondogs and reach the final of the "TV Star Search" talent contest at the Hippodrome Theatre in Ardwick. A couple of months after the group's formation Stuart Sutcliffe, a friend of John's from school, becomes the bass player.

1960

May. Among the new names suggested for Johnny and the Moondogs, Sutcliffe comes up with The Beetles, in honour of Buddy Holly's Crickets: but John argues for Beatles with its play on words.

1961

August. The German Polydor releases a single by Tony Sheridan and the Beat Brothers: the sessions include "My Bonnie," "Ain't She Sweet" sung by John and "Cry for a Shadow" written by Lennon and Harrison.

1962

23 August. He marries Cynthia Powell, whom he met at Art School. McCartney is best man.

1963

8 April. Julian Lennon is born in Liverpool.

1964

23 March. The first book of Lennon's short stories, *In His Own Write*, is published.

1 April. He meets his father for the first time in nearly twenty years, a reunion that lasts for just twenty minutes and at which Ringo and Paul are also present.

1965

24 June. He publishes his second book, *A Spaniard in the Works*.
13 July. Lennon and McCartney win the prestigious Ivor Novello Award, an important British recognition of literary quality in song lyrics. They win the following year as well, on 11 July 1966.

1966

July-September. He is on the set of the first film in which he has a starring role: *How I Won the War*, directed by Richard Lester, is being made in Spain and Germany. During the shooting he composes "Strawberry Fields Forever." In particular he will spend time in the town of Almería, staying first at a small hostel called El Delfín Verde, and then in a more spacious and suitable residence chosen by Cynthia, where he will finish the lyrics of "Strawberry Fields Forever." At Almería, where his picture is taken by the photographer Douglas Kirkland, he also celebrates his twenty-sixth birthday, with his friends from the film and others who come from England.
September. A controversial interview originally given by Lennon on 4 March to Maureen Cleave of the *Evening Standard* ("John Lennon: 'We're more popular than Jesus'") appears in the American magazine *Datebook* and provokes a fierce reaction: in the city of Birmingham, Alabama, groups of fans burn discs and memorabilia of The Beatles in public. A week later, they are banned from South African radio.

1968

1 July. John's first art exhibition: his drawings are on show at the Robert Fraser Gallery in London.
18 October. John and Yoko are arrested for possession of marijuana.
8 November. After going to live with Yoko Ono, in Ringo Starr's flat on Montague Square, John gets divorced from Cynthia, who will be given custody of their son Julian.
11 November. Release of John and Yoko's album *Unfinished Music No. 1: Two Virgins*: it is an experimental work, with a variety of sound effects, and has a picture of the artists completely naked on the cover. It will be sold in a plain brown paper envelope.
11–12 December. John and Yoko are guests of the *Rock and Roll Circus*, an event organized by The Rolling Stones and originally intended for broadcast on TV but released much later as a film: they will appear in a

couple of sessions along with Keith Richards, Eric Clapton and Mitch Mitchell of the Jimi Hendrix Experience.
18 December. Happening staged by John and Yoko, who attend the pre-Christmas press conference of the Underground Art Movement inside a large white sack.

1969

20 March. John and Yoko get married in Gibraltar, at the offices of the British consulate.
25–31 March. To celebrate their marriage John and Yoko organize a sensational event at the Hilton Hotel in Amsterdam: the "bed-in," in which for a week they receive friends, reporters and colleagues in bed, in room 902.
22 April. On the roof of the Apple Corps building, on Savile Row, Lennon changes his name by deed poll. On official documents, from then on, it will no longer written as John Winston Lennon, but as John Winston Ono Lennon.
May. Produced by Zapple, the experimental department of Apple, *Unfinished Music No. 2: Life with Lions* is released: on one side are live recordings, while on the other there are the tapes made at the Queen Charlotte Hospital in London where Yoko had been admitted following a miscarriage.
26 May–2 June. The "bed-in" is repeated in Montreal, in room 1742 of the Queen Elizabeth Hotel. During these days the song "Give Peace a Chance" is recorded, with the participation of Allen Ginsberg, Timothy Leary and Petula Clark.
1 July. Road accident at Golspie, in Scotland: John, Yoko, Julian and Kyoto, the Japanese artist's daughter from her first marriage, are injured and require a number of stitches.
12–13 September. John is the protagonist of the Toronto Rock and Roll Revival: the album, attributed to the Plastic Ono Band (*Live Peace in Toronto 1969*), comes out in December. Also on the bill of the show at the Varsity Stadium are Chuck Berry, Jerry Lee Lewis and Gene Vincent.
25 September. "Cold Turkey" is recorded at the Abbey Road Studios.
25 November. He returns his MBE medal to protest against Britain's involvement in the Nigerian Civil War and the crisis in Biafra.
15 December. John's last live appearance on British soil: he takes part in the UNICEF "Peace for Christmas" benefit concert at the Lyceum Ballroom in London. Pre-Christmas pacifist announcement, in newspapers and on billboards in twelve cities around the world: "War Is Over – If You Want It." In the meantime Lennon's avant-garde disc *The Wedding Album* is also released.

1970

15 January. John's erotic lithographs *Bag One* are exhibited at the London Arts Gallery. The day after the police confiscate eight of them on the grounds of indecency.

26 January. With the help of Phil Spector, he writes and records "Instant Karma" in one day: George Harrison is on guitar.

March. John and Yoko begin a course of intensive therapy with the psychiatrist Dr Arthur Janov, founder of the controversial Primal Scream movement, who advocates regression to childhood in order to re-establish a healthy inner equilibrium. Lennon is inspired to compose several new songs by the experience.

15 May. Two short avant-garde films by John and Yoko, *Apotheosis* and *Fly*, are shown at the Cannes Festival.

6 June. John and Yoko are guests of Frank Zappa and the Mothers of Invention at their concert at Fillmore East in New York.

10 December. John is on the bill of the concert in support of the activist and "subversive" John Sinclair, held at the Chrysler Arena in Michigan.

December. In an apartment in Greenwich Village, New York, the long interview with Jann Wenner, editor of *Rolling Stone*, comes to a close. It will be published in book form under the title *Lennon Remembers* in 2000.

1971

January. *John Lennon and the Plastic Ono Band* is the album that places most emphasis on John's family trauma. "Mother" will enter the singles charts.

1 July. He records "Imagine" at his Tittenhurst Park home: the title song is inspired by a poem in Yoko's book *Grapefruit*. He also writes "God Save Us/Do the Oz" in support of the counterculture magazine *Oz*.

13 August. He flies from Heathrow Airport in London to New York: he will never set foot on British soil again.

11 September. He and Yoko appear on the American TV programme *The Dick Cavett Show*.

30 October. The LP *Imagine* tops the charts in the US and Great Britain.

17 December. He takes part in a concert at the Apollo Theatre in New York in support of the families of prisoners in the Attica Correctional Facility and the victims of the uprising there in September.

1972

29 January. Elephant's Memory is John's new backing group.

15–18 February. A guest on the *Mike Douglas Show*, John is involved in a jam session with Chuck Berry, his hero from the rock-and-roll era.

4 March. Senator Thurmond declares that Lennon should be deported from the United States for his political ideas and his links with dangerous elements like the "radicals" Abbie Hoffman and Jerry Rubin.

30 August. With two concerts at Madison Square Garden (afternoon and evening), John and Yoko raise 250,000 dollars in aid of children with mental difficulties. At the end of the second "One to One" concert, as they were billed, he is joined by Stevie Wonder and Roberta Flack in singing "Give Peace a Chance."

23 December. The documentary *Imagine* and Yoko Ono's film *Fly* are broadcast on American TV.

1973

April. John and Yoko buy an apartment in the Dakota Building, Central Park West, New York.

October. John moves for several months to Los Angeles with his assistant May Pang, for a period of separation from Yoko. In the meantime he records *Rock 'n' Roll* with Phil Spector, a disc paying homage to the great musicians of the fifties. After some trouble over the tapes, which had disappeared because of misunderstandings with Spector, the project will see the light of day in March 1975.

1 November. The album *Mind Games* is released.

1974

April. He produces *Pussycats*, the album of his friend Harry Nilsson. In August he will give Ringo a hand, writing and playing on the track "Goodnight Vienna" on the album of the same name.

1 August. Recording of *Walls and Bridges* at the Record Plant in New York: John has written the ten songs in a week. Among those who participate in the sessions are Julian, aged eleven, on drums, Nilsson and Elton John.

28 November. The last live concert: at Madison Square Garden in New York, with Elton John as guest. They play three songs together, "Whatever Gets You Through the Night," "Lucy in the Sky with Diamonds" and "I Saw Her Standing There" (which will be released on an EP, in March 1981).

1975

31 January. John and Yoko are reunited and he returns to New York.

13 June. Lennon's last appearance on television, when he performs "Imagine" and "Slippin' and Slidin'" on the programme *A Salute to Sir Lew Grade*.

20 September. David Bowie's "Fame," written in collaboration with Lennon and Carlos Alomar, is at the top of the singles charts. John has contributed to the album *Young Americans*, as well as playing guitar on Bowie's version of "Across the Universe."

5 October. The Court of Appeals overturns the order for Lennon's deportation from the United States.

9 October. Sean Taro Ono Lennon is born in New York, on John's thirty-fifth birthday. For the next five years John will devote almost all his time to his infant son.

22 November. The compilation album *Shaved Fish* climbs the British charts and "Imagine" comes out for the first time as a single.

1976

26 July. His request for a permit of residence in the US is granted.

1977

30 January. He attends President Jimmy Carter's Inaugural Ball at the White House.

May. He pays Big Seven Music 6,795 dollars for the improper use of a piece by Chuck Berry, "You Can't Catch Me," in one part of "Come Together."

1980

1 June. He travels by sailboat to Bermuda and starts to write new songs. Recording sessions at the Hit Factory studios in New York from 4 August to 10 September.

2 September. He signs with Geffen Records.

23 October. The single "(Just Like) Starting Over" is released.

29 November. *Double Fantasy* marks John's return to making albums: the title comes from the name of a flower he saw in a botanical garden in Bermuda.

8 December. John is murdered by a young fan, the twenty-five-year-old Mark Chapman, who shoots him four times with a pistol at the entrance to his New York home, at 10:30 pm. His death, from loss of blood, is declared an hour later at Roosevelt Hospital. By the end of the month *Double Fantasy* tops the charts all over the world.

1981

25 August. Chapman is given a sentence of 20 years to life for Lennon's murder. He will be denied parole many times.

1982

24 February. While John is celebrated at the Brit Awards in London for his contribution to British music, *Double Fantasy* is named "Album of the Year" at the Grammy Awards.

1984

January. Release of the *Milk and Honey* album with new songs (six by John and six by Yoko) and of *Heart Play – Unfinished*

Dialogue, which includes extracts from the interview Lennon granted to *Playboy*.

21 March. Julian, Sean and Yoko attend the opening of the Strawberry Fields memorial in Central Park.

November. Julian Lennon, whose similarity in appearance and voice to his father has been noted by many, achieves his first hit with "Too Late for Goodbyes," from the album *Valotte*.

1985

29 June. The Rolls-Royce Phantom 5 that used to belong to John Lennon and is painted with psychedelic designs is sold for 2,299,000 dollars at an auction in New York.

1986

November. Release of the album *Menlove Avenue*, whose title comes from the name of the street in Liverpool on which John grew up. The disc contains previously unreleased takes from the *Rock 'n' Roll* and *Walls and Bridges* sessions.

1988

September. Yoko produces a series of radio broadcasts with Lennon interviews and auditions and denounces Albert Goldman's biography, which she considers offensive to John's memory.

4 October. *Imagine*, a film with a soundtrack by Lennon, is shown in New York.

1989

18 January. John is inducted into the Rock and Roll Hall of Fame as a member of The Beatles: Yoko and Sean attend the ceremony in New York.

April. Cynthia Lennon opens Lennon's Restaurant in London, with dishes like Sgt. Pepper Steak and Penny Lane Pâté on menu.

May. *Imagine: John Lennon* and *Sweet Toronto* come out on videocassette.

1990

5 May. Grand celebratory concert, ten years after his death, at the Pier Head Arena of Liverpool, with proceeds going to the Spirit Foundation. Among the artists singing John's songs are Al Green, Joe Cocker, Lenny Kravitz, Kylie Minogue, Natalie Cole, Ringo Starr, Tom Petty, the Moody Blues, Lou Reed, Randy Travis, Cyndi Lauper, Dave Stewart, Ray Charles, Daryl Hall and John Oates.

9 October. "Imagine" is sung simultaneously in a hundred and thirty countries to mark what would have been Lennon's fiftieth birthday.

30 October. Release of *Lennon*, a boxed set of four CDs with seventy-three songs from John's solo career.

21–22 December. A double tribute concert to Lennon at the Tokyo Dome in Japan: performers include Miles Davis, Linda Ronstadt, Hall & Oates and Sean Lennon.

1992

7 May. Christie's auction house sells a leather jacket that belonged to John for 43,500 dollars.

16 July. *Imagine: The John Lennon Story* opens at the Liverpool Playhouse: forty-six songs are performed, and the actor playing the role of the singer is Mike McGann. The musical is based on an idea from Bob Eaton, who had produced the documentary *Lennon* in 1986.

1994

19 January. At the annual ceremony of induction into the Rock and Roll Hall of Fame at the Waldorf Astoria in New York, Lennon enters the pantheon of contemporary music in the role of "solo artist."

1995

28 October. *Working Class Hero – A Tribute to John Lennon* appears in the shops and the charts, with performances by the Red Hot Chili Peppers, Mary Chapin Carpenter, Flaming Lips, Cheap Trick, George Clinton and others.

1998

21 March. The compilation *Lennon Legend: The Very Best of John Lennon*, with the artist's twenty most popular songs, enters the charts.

7 May. Sean Lennon makes his debut in London, at the Barfly in Camden Town, performing the songs on *Into the Sun*, his first album made with his Japanese girlfriend Yuka Honda, of the group Cibo Matto.

14 November. The quadruple CD *Anthology* that proposes different phases of Lennon's artistic career attracts strong interest. The first disc, *Ascot*, includes demos made at home, in his house in Berkshire; *New York City* refers to tracks laid down in the Big Apple; *The Lost Weekend* is mostly made up of tapes recorded in Los Angeles and New York in 1994; while *Dakota* contains home recordings on which little Sean can also be heard.

2000

9 October. On the sixtieth anniversary of his birth a museum devoted entirely to John Lennon is opened in the Japanese city of Saitama: guitars, clothes, photos, autograph writings and many objects that belonged to the former Beatle are on display. The museum, conceived and inaugurated by Yoko Ono, will not have the success she hoped for: at the beginning of 2010 it is announced that it will close for good on 30 September.

8 December. On the twentieth anniversary of his death, a memorial to John Lennon is unveiled in Havana: Fidel Castro attends the ceremony.

2001

2 October. Event at the Radio City Music Hall with a self-explanatory title: "Come Together: A Night for John Lennon's Words and Music."

It is hosted by Kevin Spacey, who sings "Mind Games"; among the artists on the bill: Lou Reed, Moby, Alanis Morrissette, the Stone Temple Pilots, Dave Matthews and Natalie Merchant.

2004

2 November. An album of solo and alternative recordings by John is released with the title *Acoustic*.

2005

4 October. The double CD *Working Class Hero: The Definitive John Lennon* comes out: thirty-eight songs and two and a half hours of music.

5 December. John Lennon's entire solo catalogue is made available in digital format.

2006

15 September. Premièred at the Venice Film Festival, the documentary *The U.S. vs. John Lennon* directed by David Leaf and John Scheinfeld II is released. The film focuses on Lennon's social and political activism and his conflict with the American authorities, presenting material obtained in part through Yoko's collaboration. The DVD comes out in the US on 13 February 2007.

2007

9 October. Yoko Ono opens the Imagine Peace Tower in Reykjavik, Iceland: the work is surrounded by about half a million messages of peace that the author has collected since 1981.

2008

29 April. Eagle brings out in its Classic Album Series a DVD presenting the story and background of the disc *John Lennon and the Plastic Ono Band*.

27 May. With authorization from the Lennon Estate, Ben & Jerry introduces a new flavour of ice cream: Imagine Whirled Peace.

2009

26 December. World première in Great Britain of the film *Nowhere Boy* that its director Sam Taylor Wood has devoted to Lennon and in particular to his adolescence and the foundation of his first group, The Quarrymen. Aaron Johnson plays the main role.

2010

16 February. On Yoko Ono's initiative, the Plastic Ono Band reunites for one night, at the BAM in New York: in addition to Sean, friends from yesterday and today took to the stage: Eric Clapton, Klaus Voorman, Bette Midler, Paul and Harper Simon, Martha Wainwright and others.

5 October. In concomitance with the "Gimme Some Truth" campaign, Lennon's eight solo albums are reissued along with three others, comprising a total of 121 remastered tracks and including various rarities. In particular *Double Fantasy* is released in a double CD version.

Cinecolor Intervalo • no. 55 • Editorial Columba • Argentina • 1986

JOHN LENNON, SIMBOLO DE UNA ERA

Por Pedro M.Mazzino
Dibujos de Rezzónico
Portada:Mario Ciurca

110

Y tienen razón. Ahora es cuando comienzo a ser yo mismo, Yoko. Necesitaba nuevas ideas.

¡Esa oriental lo asfixia con sus extravagantes teorías! ¡Dejó de hacer música y se ha puesto a pintar tonterías!

¿Qué pasaría si John conociera tus opiniones, Paul?

Acabo de conocerlas, Ringo. Y no me asombran. En una mente vulgar sólo penetran pensamientos vulgares. Pero la vida es demasiado corta para pelearse con los amigos.

Vives demasiado preocupado por tu imagen, Paul. Lo más importante es hacer lo que a uno le plazca y divertirse. Eso también me lo enseñó Yoko Ono.

Ringo Star se adaptó enseguida a la nueva situación. Sus fiestas en la mansión de Marble Arch se caracterizaron por lo ruidosas y el escándalo atrajo a la prensa. Los excesos iban en aumento.

¡Lee lo que dicen de los Beatles, John! ¡Nos consideran en plena decadencia!

"Olvíd... comien... licle y h... vivo para... se con lo... discos...

...nes "comenza... ...o eran los re... ...op. La pelícu... ...ompimiento ...e el propio ...nció.

Me culpan, John. Dicen que logré desunirlos metiéndome todo el tiempo en las cosas del grupo.

Olvídalo, Yoko. Ellos no saben todo lo que representas para mí.

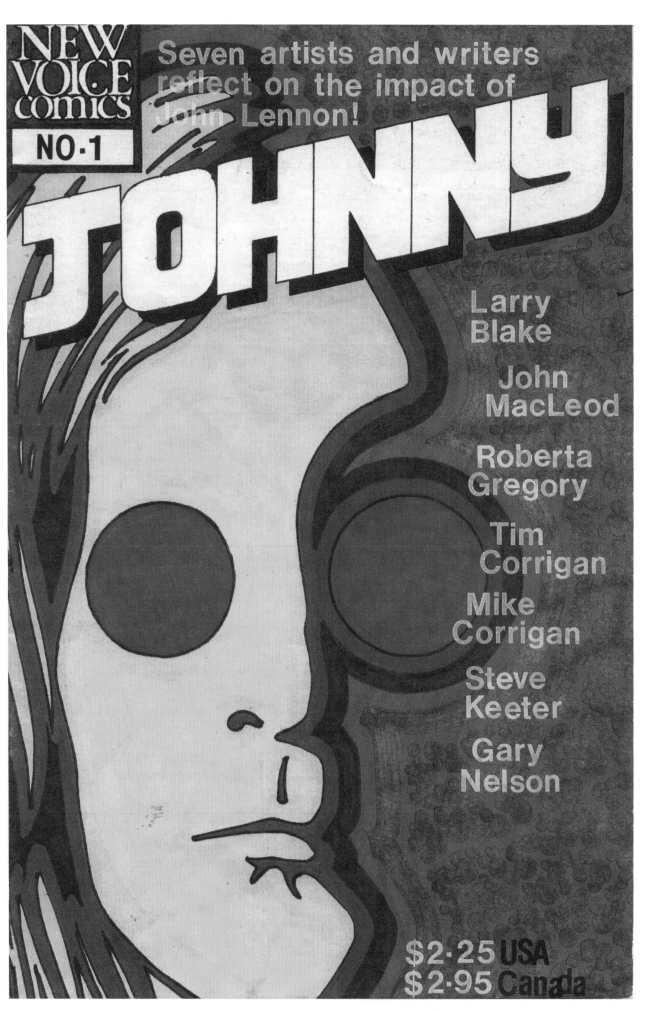